Bevitized!

CELEBRATING YOU-NIQUENESS
IN A COOKIE CUTTER
WORLD

By Beverly Schatz

Dedication

My mother, Marie, celebrated my "You-niqueness" better than anyone I have ever known. Her patience, love and understanding for a child that was not at all sure she would ever want to venture into the world was extraordinary. She passed away in April of 2016 so even though she won't be able to celebrate this accomplishment with me, I feel it is only right to dedicate my very first book to her. Not all mothers would have had the patience to wash their child's sheets every morning, never scolding their child for wetting the bed. Not all mothers would have driven their child to school every day because their child was afraid to ride the bus. Not all mothers would have graduated from kindergarten for their little five year old while their terrified five year old waited in the car and surely not all mothers would have allowed their child to go to first grade every day after PE was over because all those gymnastics stunts scared her first grader even more than that terrifying graduation ceremony the year before. I'm sure she had moments when she wondered if I would turn out somewhat normal but loved me regardless. She offered the purest, most precious unconditional love a child could ever experience. She was selfless, kind and celebrated every "You-nique" quality I possessed. I miss her physical presence so very much but in my heart I know, she is always by my side.

1

Foreword

The writer and author of this masterpiece is my wife. She wasn't my wife the first time I read her writing, but rather a woman who had just entered into my life in a less common or shall I say technological way. Some of my first reads were her jots of news for several newspapers and exchanged emails in our whirlwind online romance. Friends, family, co-workers and I became subjects for the stories that would transpire! Her mother would have loved to read every word and discuss and laugh at all the fun, exciting and real life memories written in Bev's unique way.

I can say that my wife (I married this beautiful, caring and creative woman) tells a true story when the time is "write."

Sit down and enjoy life's stories through the eyes of the most creative person I have ever known!

Preface

I believe every person in this world is here for a reason. We all have a unique set of qualities that makes us who we are. I also believe there is a reason for every obstacle and triumph we encounter. The obstacles strengthen our weaknesses and force us to grow beyond what we believed possible. Our triumphs are the moments filled with joy when we've pushed ourselves and learned that there is always more within us until there isn't.

We will all reach the end of our journey and we'll all find out if what we believed is what is. I believe in God. I believe that Mary, The Blessed Virgin, did indeed, give birth to Jesus. I believe He is the Son of God and that He died on the cross for us. I realize not everyone believes what I believe. That is your choice.

The world seems so out of balance at times but it doesn't have to change who we are. It was once said that in the forces of good and evil only one can survive and the one that survives is the one you feed. I choose to feed the force that inspires others, warms hearts, lightens loads and the one that genuinely cares about the well-being of the many people I have had the pleasure of knowing.

Introduction

I grew up in a very tiny town in the northeast corner of South Dakota. I had two hard working parents that created a very stable environment for my older sister, my older brother and me. We learned the value of a dollar at a very early age and started doing odd jobs that brought about the funding necessary for treasures like mood rings and clock radios purchased at the tiny little "general" store that was a two minute bike ride away from our house. As time went on we entered adulthood and the odd jobs became full time jobs that paid bills and bought homes that provided a sense of security and wellbeing we once enjoyed under our parents' roof. After graduating with honors from high school I probably should have gone on to college but decided not to. Instead I worked some part time jobs, married the wrong man and learned that life is full of choices and challenges. I learned that the challenges present some very difficult decisions and the choices aren't always as clear as we would like them to be but at the end of every day, if we're paying attention, there is always something to be thankful for.

About 5 years ago I started jotting down a few thoughts and over time those thoughts turned into walks down memory lane, strides through difficult times, reflections on aging parents, commentary on customers, marches through marital bliss and every thought that transpired helped me to realize just how unique we all really are. We look different, we talk different, we have different opinions and that seemingly unending thought is, in fact, unending.

It wasn't long before I realized I had developed a passion for writing and when shared, I learned that my choice of words tends to invite readers to go right along with me and my thoughts. My inspiration is sparked sometimes by the smallest details included in the credits of an ordinary day while other times it's ignited by experiences brought about by circumstances a bit more unusual and unexpected.

Bevitized! is a collection of short stories. They're not in any particular order. There are stories that transpired before my parents passed away, whimsical humor from my childhood days, revelations from marriage number one and marriage number "I finally got this right" as well as a great assortment of inspiration that took root and grew while I managed custom frame shops, inspired creativity at fabric stores, sorted mail and managed post offices, worked as a florist, managed a c-store and booked reservations at a hotel. My life has not been boring. I've met a lot of interesting people and not one of them fit into the "cookie cutter" mentality we're forced to be a part of when we make our way into the world!

I so hope you enjoy this journey. If I did, indeed, accomplish what I set out to do, you will laugh, be inspired, shed a tear and realize you may not have wrinkles on your forehead just like I don't or have a big sister that couldn't spell "blood" in third grade just like me or hated weeding a mile long row of green beans just like me but that you are "You-nique" just like you and you're worth celebrating!

Thank Your Mom

Because of the fact that Bevitized is dedicated to my amazing mom, I felt that my first story should be one inspired by her. She was always busy and set an amazing example of how a household should be run. She made a list of things she planned to accomplish every day and every day her list was accomplished. I remember visiting with her a few days before she passed away and she said, "I have always made a list of things to do every day but I haven't lately." She hesitated for a few seconds, took a breath and then said, "I guess I got everything done." I'll probably never forget that moment as it helped me to realize how hard it is to be an adult with an aging parent that you know you will have to let go of much sooner than you'd like because they have "everything done." Here's a reflection that might inspire patience and selfless love for someone in your life that has nearly "everything done" as well.

Be thankful for all those times you watched as your mom cleaned your room and picked up your toys because you wouldn't, even after she reminded you 10 times. You'll be referencing her behavior down the road when her knees will no longer allow her to bend over far enough to reach the floor.

Be thankful for all those times your mom zipped your coat before you went outside to play in the snow. You'll know just what to do when she can no longer wrap her swollen, arthritic fingers around that tiny little tab dangling at the end of her zipper.

Be thankful she was there every time you woke up to comfort you when you had a bad dream. She's going to need to be comforted too but the bad things she has to face won't be a dream.

Be thankful that she loved you no matter what. There will come a time in her life when she won't be nearly as easy to love as she was when you were a kid, but you'll love her anyway.

Be thankful for all the times she fixed what you broke, kissed what you bumped and forgot your mistakes. Down the road, things will change and you'll see things break and one of those things will be your heart as you watch your mother struggle with everything that used to be so easy.

Be thankful for all those times you managed to slip away from the table after supper without helping with the dishes. You will eventually have a sink full of dirty dishes when she's not there and you'll realize all those dirty dishes you walked away from when you were a kid didn't actually wash themselves.

Be thankful for the strength in your hands, especially the one you write with. There may come a time in your life when that strength you've always known unexpectedly leaves you and you spend the better part of an hour addressing an envelope that used to take seconds.

Be thankful for all those times your mother had to remind you to do something even though you really hadn't forgotten about it. You were just "putting it off" as long as possible because kids are like that. There may come a time you'll have to remind your mother to do almost everything and often times, more than once, because she really isn't "putting it off." It's because she really doesn't remember.

Be thankful for all those times when your mother stayed up waiting for you to return home safely. You were a teenager and you knew everything and you thought it was just stupid for her to worry. There may come a time when you'll find yourself lying awake wondering if she's safe and warm and comfortable because you know you can't be with her as often as she'd like.

Be thankful for your mother if your mother was like mine. She was one of the most selfless human beings I have ever known and my love for her is immeasurable. As time went on she was slowly being forced to let go of the independence she had enjoyed for years and not a moment went by that I didn't worry about her, that was, until she was safely Home.

Snoring On A Resume?

Several years ago my beloved husband suffered some irreversible back damage as the result of a car accident. Unfortunately he has nights when his back pain keeps him awake and quite restless. I usually go to bed later than him as I'm more of a Moon Flower in the garden of life and he's the Morning Glory. This gives him the chance to fall sound asleep before I attempt to do the same but a while back things happened in reverse. I fell asleep first and learned later that insomnia decided to play a dirty little trick on my exhausted husband. It wanted to discuss plans of what the morning glory was going to do the following day, when he was going to take the feather pillows in to be fluffed and lots of other things that kept the eye on the left and the eye on the right side of Donald's head wide open! I, on the other hand, was apparently lying flat on my back, most likely dreaming that I was arm knitting a scarf made out of yarn spun from the looms of leprechauns and I had no idea my other half was awake. All of a sudden, from out of nowhere, he successfully delivered the nudge of all nudges and woke me up to stop what I'm sure was a very feminine, nearly undetectable noise some

9

might refer to as snoring. He considered it a 'gentle nudge" but my brain said, "Put down your damn yarn woman! The house is ON FIRE!!! After the initial shock of being woke up from a very sound sleep, I let my heart talk me into letting it get below 155 beats per minute. Next, I checked to make sure neither Donald nor I were actually on fire and then performed a complete investigation of the house after I piled out of bed and walked rather abruptly down the hall muttering something like, "You won't be getting another chance to do that in the near future because I will be knitting…err…I mean sleeping on the couch!" I often wonder if it is at all possible to wake someone from a sound sleep like that without causing them to be violently alarmed. From my experience, I have not yet seen a different reaction than mine, ever but then, I have only witnessed mine. It's still statistical information and made this part of the story interesting, don't you think? Usually I'm not the "huffy" type but that night, I had a wrong way and it got rubbed! Apparently, I WAS emitting a very soft, feminine, almost undetectable amount of noise that some might refer to as snoring. I'm not sure why women hate to believe they snore but according to my source, I do and it doesn't appear to be all that soft or feminine and it's safe to say I could add it to my resume as it is allegedly something I'm quite good at! My husband snores a lot, but I've trained my brain to interpret it as one of those soothing sounds you would hear on one of those relaxation machines. It works great as it requires no batteries, no electricity and it's very reliable.... that is, if it doesn't have insomnia!

The Season Before Spring

Don't you just love that time of year when you know you have to start assembling the necessary paperwork needed to begin your tax return? Yeah, me neither. For me it isn't all that hard to locate the paperwork I need as I have a somewhat organized filing system AND it usually doesn't take very long AND I usually get a refund BUT I still drag my feet. Perhaps there is a tiny, microscopic, nearly undetectable bit of procrastinator in me but please don't tell my husband. His chest would swell up and every button on his shirt would pop off if he heard I admitted this and then I would have to work around his buttonless shirt on my sewing table for months before I actually took the time to sew the buttons back on!

Let's move on to my favorite "tax season" story. It will help to distract you just in case you run into my husband and decide to tell him that I may have admitted to a bit of truth in his procrastination theory. This memory might also put a smile on your face and if not, it will certainly offer some very good advice of what not to do while you are sitting in your accountant's office.

It was a number of years ago that I made my yearly appointment with the guy at the bank that prepared tax returns after hours. He was a very pleasant man and his wife would usually stay in the office with him as she did a portion of the paperwork as well. It became rather routine after the first couple of years. I would go in with my W-2 and an assortment of receipts and some numbers from my little crafting business. He would finger through them and ask a few questions and every year it was quite uneventful, that is, until the year I decided to look down at the floor while he was going over my receipts. Typically, during this part of the visit there was a bit of silence. I struggle with

11

silence. I just love talking so much! Conversations are the word bouquets of life! However, I knew he needed to concentrate and so I tried to occupy my thoughts with a quick look around the office. I thought about how I would probably paint the walls a different color and rearrange the desks and then, that one particular year, just as I began to explore flooring options for my interior design strategy of this office space my eyes attached a glue-like gaze to something down towards the end of my pant leg. I should have just ignored it but the harder I tried, the more curious I got. What is it? I managed to override the desire to investigate for a while and continued on with my hypothetical renovation plans but eventually that ridiculous curiosity got the best of me and I bent over, ever so slowly and took a hold of the mystery and gave it a pull. Unfortunately, I was not able to make it as unnoticeable as I had originally planned and before I knew it, there was an entire sock in my hand! I suppose we've all had spare socks statically attach themselves to various parts of our clothing at times, but I would also be willing to bet those items are usually discovered before you leave the house! Needless to say, I was immediately struck with bouts of uncontrollable laughter. I laughed the rest of the time I was there, all the way to my car and all the way home. It was somewhat unfortunate for the accountant and his wife, but I must say it makes "tax season" just a bit less taxing every time I think about my stowaway sock. I may have possibly solved the age-old missing sock mystery once blamed on the dryer. Now we know, the dryer doesn't eat the socks, it just hides them in places you might not think to look until you're deciding which flooring would work best with the paint color you secretly chose for the walls in your accountant's office while he was making sure he had all the information he was going to need to proceed with your tax return! I was sort of curious how the conversation between him and his wife went after I left as bouts of laughter that cause snorting and tears probably weren't behaviors they typically witnessed when it came to preparing tax returns!

Pushed Pins

A few weeks ago I met a young woman that started working where I find myself 40 hours a week. She was very tall and thin. I would guess her to be around 22 years old and she had two of the saddest eyes I have ever seen. Over the course of the very short amount of time I worked with her I made several attempts to get to know her but always felt as if the wall she surrounded herself with was not going to be an easy one to break through. I've learned that taking your time with someone like this is important so I distanced myself a bit but never missed an opportunity to say hello. A few days passed and when I went to count the bank deposit after she finished preparing it I thought. "I still haven't made a connection with her. What can I do?" I turned in the office chair to the hook the cash bag hangs on and I saw an opportunity. There were several push pins on the bulletin board completely out of work so I decided to arrange them in the shape of a happy face. I thought, "When she returns from the bank to hang up the bag she'll surely see that face smiling at her and maybe it will make her smile back." I felt as if there had to be a way to break into the vault those sad eyes held the combination for.

Unfortunately my attempt to make her feel just a bit happy didn't get a chance to work. When she returned from the bank she tossed the deposit bag on the counter in the office and walked out leaving her resignation on the manager's desk. She didn't offer the typical two weeks' notice but rather told us she had no plans of returning the following day. I was really hoping for an opportunity to "reach" her but that opportunity never took root and never had the chance to grow. God knew I tried though; I know He did.

I had a terrible day at work yesterday. I don't have lots of them, thank goodness but I do have them and when I do I can never just let it go. I dissect the details that caused my frustration and even attempt to convince myself of a different outcome. I dread the following day as it seems there is almost always repercussions that surface that tend to reignite the flames from the prior day. I asked God to help me through the "aftershock" period but if you're like me you find yourself wondering if He did, indeed, hear you. I don't always pick up on His signs to reassure me that things are going to be okay so with a bit of hesitation I walked out the door to face my impending fears.

I didn't go to work right away as I had an obligation for work at another address first which helped to calm my ability to overthink what would happen when I did actually get to work. After about an hour and a half I finished my tasks and as I walked down the hall to leave something convinced me to look up before turning the corner and on the bulletin board right in front of me there was a face created from push pins smiling at me! It was on the lower right corner of that bulletin board which just happened to be the very same corner I had arranged push pins on the bulletin board at work only days before! I had walked past that bulletin board at the end of the hall so many times before but the decision to look up today could not have happened at a better time.

We never have to wonder if God hears us when we pray but we do. We never have to bear a burden alone but feeling alone feels very real sometimes and we never have to wonder if attempting to brighten someone's day is a good idea even if they don't realize you tried because there will come a time in your life when you'll know your prayers are heard, that you're not alone and that Someone may attempt to brighten your day in a "push pin" kind of way!

Hazardous Discoveries

Not because I was trying in any way, but I have discovered a brand-new way to be 100% awake and more alert than I ever imagined possible with that very first step out of bed. It works better than Folgers in my cup. It works better than having someone give me a "THE HOUSE IS ON FIRE!" shake and even better than having cold water dumped on my head. It's not complicated and there are no expensive supplies to purchase. If you have a really bad memory like me, you can install it yourself the night before but if your memory is sharp you'll need someone to set up this proven method of miraculous consciousness for you but trust me, it works!

Okay, now that I've aroused your curiosity let me tell you what happened and how this newly found sensation came to be. It was Valentine's Day and my husband, who had been out of town for work, told me that he was on his way home to spend the evening with me. I was excited but realized I needed to get his gift wrapped and set up the unique way I thought he should find it. I gathered my supplies and first I slid some "gigantic bubble" variety bubble wrap under the throw that was stretched across our bed where he would sit down to open his gift. This would give things a little "fireworks" sort of flair when he plopped down, I thought. I placed his gift on top of the throw near where he would be sitting along with his card and two balloons and then scattered chocolate hearts all around. Lastly, I took a roll of curling ribbon and taped one end to his gift and then proceeded to unroll the ribbon throughout the house ending up by the front door that he would be walking through in just a few short minutes. I taped a note to the ribbon that read, "Follow me baby!" He's a pretty good sport when it comes to my hi-jinks, so when he walked through the door he started his adventure with the ribbon that led him into the living room, then the dining room and then to the kitchen, hallway, bathroom, spare bedroom and finally to our bedroom. So he wouldn't miss out on the "fireworks" part I put a sign on the bed where I wanted him to sit that read, "Butt goes here." He found this quite amusing but when he plopped down nothing happened. For a second I entertained thoughts of asking him if he wanted to jump on the bed but my fuddy duddy adult brain took over before that "5 year old Bev" still hiding somewhere inside my head slipped out. (Note to self: mattresses are soft you idiot! Throw the cutting board and then the bubble wrap under throw next time!) He loved his card, his gift, the balloons and the chocolates and didn't know anything about the fizzled fireworks. We shared some hugs and kisses and then went into the dining room to enjoy some fabulous grilled steaks. We played cards and consumed a few adult beverages and around midnight we headed to bed. His gifts were still there so I gathered them up and took them into the kitchen. We crawled into bed and the next thing we knew; it was morning. He got up and headed to the bathroom. Morning types do this without issues. This is NOT me. I was still a bit groggy but I sat up and slid my legs over the side of the bed. My left foot decided to go first. My right foot followed and then…FIREWORKS!!!! The explosion that took place once my feet hit the floor nearly put me in an early grave! I had forgotten all about that crazy bubble wrap I had slipped under the throw the night before and while we slept it found its way to the floor and waited patiently for me to "light the fuse!!!"

They say some of the best inventions happen by accident. I'll bet statistically; emergency rooms meet a lot of inventors!

It's Not On The Menu

When we were kids, dad would load us up in the back of the pickup, throw some big 5-gallon buckets in with us and we would head out to find some plum trees loaded with big, juicy plums that mom would use to make jelly. I remember how amazing those buckets of plum would smell sitting out in the entry way and how wonderful they smelled while they were cooking. My sister and brother-in-law remembered this too and one year, they decided to toss a few plums in the freezer to use as potpourri on Christmas day. They thought the smell of plums cooking would surely fill their kitchen with a very good memory for all of us. What they didn't know is that it would "create" a great memory rather than spark one from our past.

Christmas day arrived and the plums were extracted from the freezer and placed in a small saucepan with a little water and put on the stove to simmer. Once they began to cook, they popped open and the bright yellow pulp inside began to fill the pan and they took on a much different appearance than a pan filled with plums. What transpired as the evening went on still makes me hysterical.

The family began to show up and once we are all present and accounted for, we were told it was time to get in line and load up our plates. There were tons of delectable choices and as we walked along, I spotted the pan on the stove and my brain said, "Aw look, sweet potatoes!" and proceeded to tell my husband he better not forget to take some as they're one of his favorite dishes. He listened and we headed to the table to enjoy the wonderful Christmas supper my sister had prepared. There were conversations spilling from the corners of every food filled mouth and laughter all around but none that would compare to the laughter that was about to transpire. We had all reached a point where we were in that "should I go back for seconds?" or "I think I'm ready for dessert" phase when my eyes caught sight of something quite unusual. My husband's plate didn't have that "completely empty and licked clean" look like it always did when he ate. It had a tiny pile of pits on it. I asked him where he got the pits and he said, "They were in the sweet potatoes." Unfortunately, my laughter could not be contained and before long everyone knew he had consumed a rather substantial amount of the "potpourri!"

The Dressing Gamble

I no longer get ready for work in the dark. Years ago I did this quite often and I think it had something to do with the fact that I have never been much of a morning person and I suppose I thought that if I didn't turn the light on while I was getting dressed my brain would, in some way, think it was still sleeping. I know this doesn't make any sense, but I was in my early twenties and it made sense to me, up until one particular day. I had decided to wear my bright turquoise dress with the black button trim. I reached in my drawer and pulled out a pair of dark colored nylons and proceeded to assemble myself for the long day ahead. Once the clothes were in place, I reluctantly turned on the light in my bedroom so that I could curl my hair and apply my daily dose of makeup. I didn't bother to do a final inspection before leaving but felt pretty confident I was one coordinated kind of gal. I'm not sure why but some outfits give you sort of a lift. For me it's typically an outfit where everything flows like this one. I loved my black and turquoise dress and my black nylons and black flats. Together they gave me that "I can take on the world!" kind of feeling. This stellar woman went strolling into work as if she owned the place! After several hours on the retail floor I headed back to take a break and it was one of those breaks where you sit down on one chair and hike your legs up on another chair and simply r-e-l-a-x. Ahhhhhh was usually the sound I would emit as it felt so good to sit down if only for a short time. The second the hiking my legs onto the other chair happened my peaceful, relaxed bliss came to a screeching halt and I almost choked on the diet coke I was taking a sip of! My dark nylons weren't black at all, they were OLIVE GREEN! Can you imagine Miss "Take on the world" wearing such a gross combination?!!! Turquoise and olive green! Yuck! I ran to the bathroom and took them off and threw them in the garbage and during my lunch break I headed to the store to buy a pair of black ones. I can honestly say I check everything very carefully now when I get dressed, just to be sure! Lesson learned: Be careful on the days you decide to hold your head up high as you might just stumble on a heaping helping of humility disguised as olive green nylons somewhere along the way!

The Camper - Part One

Several years ago, our niece came to stay for a week and right about the time she arrived my husband found out his job would be taking him out of town for a few days. Our niece and I would be all alone in the big city and the only thing standing between her and I and a ton of shopping was......well.... NOTHING! We always enjoyed each other's company as she was always game for anything. This would end up being very beneficial as what transpired was going to require at least one good sport when someone's wife got a bit perturbed! The 4th of July was not far off and my husband decided we should buy a pop-up camper. The only problem I could see with this is the fact that he wasn't home to go camper shopping. He thought Aimee and I should go and scope out the possibilities but because I hadn't lived here all that long I opted to do a bit of online research instead and located a very nice, slightly used camper. I sent him a text with pictures and he asked if I liked it. I told him it looked very nice, so he asked us to go and check it out. I called the camper store and it just so happened they had it set up and ready to view. The wind was blowing approximately 40 mph that day so I was certain the camper would be set up inside the showroom. I mean, who would be stupid enough to set up a pop-up camper in wind like that, right? Apparently, the camper store I called and when we arrived, the house on wheels was waiting patiently for us in the parking lot with no visible signs of being airborne. Aimee and I found an eager salesman that led us out to the pop-up wonder. We looked it over, snapped some pictures for Don and then asked him to show us how to "unpop" it. We told him he would most likely be hearing from us and we headed home. Don returned that evening and wasn't at all excited to hear about our detailed research. We had to drag him into the office to look at our pictures and even then, he just didn't seem interested. Oh well, I thought, it wasn't my idea anyway.

The next morning, Don had to leave for yet another job out of town but around 10 am I received a text. It looked like a picture of a document. I asked him what it was. He made me guess. I told him it looked like a bill of sale and his response was "BINGO!" That "unexcited" facade was actually used to disguise the fact that he was actually excited about what he saw from our pictures and he bought the camper! He told me we would be able to pick it up the next day and that once we picked it up that we should have the propane tank checked on it and then pick up some camper necessities. At first, I was excited as I saw it as a day filled with lots of shopping but then I realized I was picking up a camper with a pickup and I had never picked up a camper with a pickup before in my life! Holy crap! Immediately my brain said, "Aimee, we need to do a test run!" I had only been living here about a month and a half so not everything was as familiar to me as it was to Don. Aimee, being the good sport that she is, was more than okay with my plan so we hopped in the pickup and headed out of the driveway. We would need to map out a plan for the camper retrieval and then locate the gas station Don suggested for the propane tank check. He gave us directions but they didn't work as well as I had hoped. We drove and drove and drove and kept ending up on 9th street which is not where the gas station was. Aimee said, "Well, this road looks familiar. I think we've passed this hospital 350 times!" Eventually we gave up and headed home to compare Don's instructions to Google's instructions and remarkably, they were exactly the same! Go figure. Turns out, the gas station was nowhere near 9th street!

When "Pick Up The Pop-up" day arrived it was less windy, we knew where the gas station was, we knew where we were going to park the camper, we had paper plates, napkins, towels, pillows, bedding, a small oval shaped garbage can you'll hear more about later and we knew how to turn that "jiffy pop" wonder into a bedroom fit for four! It was going to be an easy less breezy kind of day.

Thankfully the salesman knew a thing or two about how to attach a camper to a pickup. I didn't and I certainly didn't need a disconnected pop-up camper rolling backwards down the highway. I can't even begin to think how I would word that text to Don. With the fear of that happening and the camper behind us, I slipped the pickup into drive and we rolled out of the parking lot. This really wasn't going to be all that bad. I could hardly tell there was anything behind us but rather than attempt any creative stunts my adult, responsible side took over and we drove directly to the gas station and filled the propane tank and then headed home. What I didn't know is we would run across a huge pile of dirt sitting in the back alley that had mysteriously appeared there while we were gone. It was NOT part of my plan. I can't get past this mountain without tipping this camper over! I sent Don a text and for some reason ALL CAPITAL LETTERS can really grab someone's attention and just like magic, my phone was ringing. He was very calm and said, "Don't worry. I asked my buddy from work to come over and back the camper in. All I ask is that you look as pathetic as possible when he gets there." THIS, I COULD DO! Our backer upper arrived and effortlessly rolled the damn camper over the dirt pile without tipping it over and in a flash the camper was right where it needed to be. Don contacted me once he felt it was safe to converse with me again and he suggested we do some popping. I thought it was a terrible idea. He's persuasive. He said it would only take 10 minutes. I caved. Aimee and I unlatched the latches and I walked to the front of the camper and hit the magic "pop up" button and just like magic, it started to open. The key word here was "started." As it turns out, the battery didn't have enough power so after 10 minutes there it sat......half open. Well, isn't this stupid. We can't close it. We can't open it and we surely can't put all the cool stuff in it. NOW WHAT?

Don called again. He said if we hooked up the battery charger it would pop right up. Okay. He was very convincing. "Where's the battery charger?" I asked. "Are you kidding me?? It's clear across town in the storage unit!" Begrudgingly I drug my unwilling feet and my choice words off to the storage unit to retrieve the charger and once I returned and once it was hooked up, the camper popped up and we were able to move in! Aimee and I had a wonderful time after the 2 HOUR and 10 minute set up and we decided it would stay SET UP until Don was able to unset it up when he returned home.

I'm not sure why, but when Don "unset" it up it seemed to go down a whole lot faster than it went up but Aimee and I never did see it go up when we went to take a look at it at the camper store. Perhaps there was a reason for that. Final thought: If you would have been in the market for a pop-up camper, and you would have been here somewhere between me "looking pathetic" and me "retrieving the battery charger," you would have gotten one helluva deal!

The Camper - Part Two

July 4th of 2014 was fast approaching. The camper was loaded with towels, plates, silverware, napkins, games, bug spray, toilet paper and enough bedding to protect us if the temps decided to drop into the single digits. It was safe to say we were ready to embark on our maiden voyage with the pop-up wonder. Rather than dive right into camper living at an actual campground we decided our first trip would land us right at the end of the sidewalk at my mom's house.

As we strolled in the driveway, the burgers were grilling, and I believe my brother made a "Griswald" reference when he caught sight of us. Don immediately began the set-up process and before we knew it, we had our accommodations for the night ready and waiting. There was only one tiny detail that needed to be addressed at that point. The temperature was approximately 150 degrees inside our home on wheels. Don is a "problem solver" kind of guy and he was able to round up an extension cord that reached from the house to the camper and before long the air conditioner was running, and things were cooling down and everything was working out really well. Unfortunately there was a circuit breaker inside the house that had different plans. Don did a short investigation and found out that the only way we would be able to keep the air conditioner running in the camper would be to talk mom out of having the TV, the radio, 8 assorted lamps, 3 ceiling lights, 2 fans and her air conditioner all running at the same time. He attempted a negotiation with mom and the agitated circuit breaker which resulted in turning off 4 lamps, 2 ceiling lights, the radio while the TV was on and the TV when the radio was on and 1 fan. This compromise appeared to be the perfect solution to our air conditioning dilemma. When it's humid and 90 degrees outside the occupants of a pop-up camper begin to feel like the kernels inside a jiffy pop pan so air conditioning is a must if you don't want anyone to explode.

Things were going great. We took turns visiting and playing games in the cool comfort of our camper all afternoon. It was such a wonderful day with family and friends. We didn't realize that when day turned into night, we would be faced with yet another dilemma. It appeared that the darkness had something to do with the air conditioner stopping again. Now what could have caused that to happen? A light bulb came on. Literally. Mom had turned the yard light on by the back door. I didn't know the air stopped out in the camper as I was in the house visiting with mom and my sister but Don is very observant and just knew this was what the problem was so he went in the entry and shut the yard light off and then slid into the house and flipped the tripped circuit breaker. The air ran for a little while and then stopped again. Don noticed the yard light was back on, so he went back to the house but this time he loosened the bulb and found a way back to the electrical box without us noticing and then went back outside. He knew he had to outsmart the switch flipper. It worked and the air came back on. Mom noticed the yard light was off again so she grabbed a new bulb and said, "Bev, I think that yard light bulb burned out. Would you put that new bulb in?" I had no idea Don had just loosened it, so I went out to put the new bulb in and found out rather quickly that the only problem was that the bulb was loose, so I tightened it. Don saw me doing this and after I went inside, he went back and loosened it yet again. My sister got sent out with the new bulb I had returned to the kitchen table to see if she could get the yard light to work and realized a quick turn on the existing bulb was all it needed to work so she too took the new bulb back in the house explaining to mom that the old bulb was working just fine. About then I left the house and strolled back down the sidewalk to see what Don was doing and he said, "Would you please stop tightening that light bulb? I keep loosening it so we can have air conditioning, but you and your sister keep screwing it back in!"

It's safe to say we survived our very first camping adventure. I was actually able to sleep all night on a mattress thinner than a grilled cheese sandwich and it was safe to say we were ready to attempt some "real" camping at a real campground!

The Camper - Part Three

It was mid-August before we realized the camper was probably very lonely. We hadn't taken it out for any adventures since the 4th of July so we decided to head to Medora for the weekend and this time we would be experiencing life at a real campground. Don knew just the one we should use as he had camped there years ago. He told me I would absolutely love it as it was filled with a lot of beautiful trees and the camping spots were very private. He said it would almost feel like we were camping all by ourselves out in the woods. Well, who would put a stop to a plan like that? It sounded like paradise and it was just waiting for us to arrive!

The day was sunny and gorgeous. It was a little windy but due to my past experience with wind and this camper, I was well aware that it had passed the "wind test" with flying colors! We were so happy to see the campground had several secluded camping spots available when we arrived. Don is very conscientious and chose a spot that would be just a short walk to the bathrooms. He's such a wonderful guy! There were paved pads to park the camper on so Don pulled up next to the spot he chose and proceeded to back the camper into the spot where we would begin the leveling process. I was so excited. This is the part where I get to stand at the back of the camper and watch the little bubble in the level. When it's in the middle, the camper is ready to be popped up! Rather than hand crank the jacks down, Don brought along his handy, dandy power tool with the jack lowering attachment and began to lower Jack #1. In a matter of seconds, he had moved on to Jack #2. I reported the bubble was not quite in the middle so after several, and I do mean several repeated trips to each side of the camper the bubble was still not in the middle. Don felt there was something just a bit strange going on then made a rather interesting discovery. He poked his head around to the back of the camper where I was standing and said, "Bev, I'm not sure what is going on with that damn bubble, but the camper wheels are no longer ON THE GROUND!!!!!" Oops! It didn't take long to realize we would either have to lower the far end of the camper a rather significant amount or sleep on the bed at the other end and make up our minds that being rammed up against the camper window like two marbles on an uneven floor would work just fine for both of us. I'm sure you've already figured out which option we chose. (I did have a bout of laughter that rendered me nearly 100% useless for around 15 minutes. My other half was not amused.)

Once the popping up and leveling tasks were complete, we decided to check out the campground bathrooms. We're still not sure just how nice they were or if they were well stocked with toilet paper because they were LOCKED! I sat in disbelief for a few minutes and attempted to figure out just how I was going to make the camping thing work for me. Lord knows most humans have to use a bathroom at least twice a day and at least one of those times on this particular day was going to be while we were in the camper. I don't like to "go" outside as things tend to splatter on shoes if you know what I mean. I told Don maybe I could sit at the picnic table and slide my back side just over the seat edge and lift my feet in the air and I was told that was just wrong. A woman in desperation has got to have a plan. Guys have much different equipment and don't understand the issues we woman face with outdoor peeing. We were planning to go into Medora for a bit of shopping before the musical later on that night so I had some time to think about what I could do. Part of my plan was to not drink anything all day. That would certainly help, right? This plan wasn't 100% reliable as that would be about the time my body decided to rid itself of some excess water weight. I was a bit distracted, but we had fun shopping and visiting with Don's sister, her boyfriend and her youngest daughter as they were also there for the weekend. As the afternoon came to a close, it was time to head back to our camper to freshen up before the steak fondue and musical that evening. We found out there was one bathroom at the very entrance of the campground that was unlocked so we both took advantage of it before and after the musical. When we returned from the musical to use the bathroom, however, we noticed how incredibly dark it was. Would you believe there wasn't a single light shining anywhere, not even the Moon? Don was a sweetheart and gave me the flashlight from the pickup when I went in the bathroom. Can you imagine how fun things would have gotten had I went into this dark unfamiliar place only to find out I was sharing it with a startled raccoon! The flashlight proved to me there were no raccoons, startled or otherwise, thank goodness, so I had the perfect opportunity to squeeze every ounce of fluid I could out of my body in hopes that I wouldn't need to worry about peeing again until the sun came up.

We managed to find our camper in what would appear to be one of the darkest nights we've ever encountered and with the assistance of the flashlight we were able to get out of the pickup and find the camper door and head inside to settle in for the night. The air conditioning on this trip was provided by Mother Nature, thank goodness, as there were also no electrical hook ups available. Big shock, right? I remember Don checking the weather on his phone and telling me it was going to be one of the coolest nights August had seen in a long time but I was ready as Aimee and I had packed enough blankets and comforters in the camper to keep us toasty no matter what. Finally, we were in bed. I was not allowing my brain to reference any word that had anything to do with having to go to the bathroom. I was not thinking about water or drinking anything. I was going to make it through the night. I kept telling myself, you can do this, you can do this and finally I was asleep. Approximately 2 hours later I'll bet you can almost guess what happened. My eyes popped open like a tightly wound spring on a window shade, and I was, indeed, awake and I had to pee! Okay, so I have to pee. What are my options? There has got to be options, right? Okay, I could go out into the black scary night and pee at the picnic table and just not tell Don but with my luck I would trip going out the camper door and break my leg. I could drive the pickup over to the entrance and use the bathroom that was unlocked or......

......I could straddle the tiny little oval shaped garbage can Aimee and I bought when we were shopping for camper supplies. Hmmm......I wonder if that would work? I could line it with several garbage bags and make sure I have the toilet paper ready in case something goes terribly wrong......yes, by golly, I think this will work!

Being resourceful is a very good thing. Having common sense is also a very good thing. Combining both will create a toilet in a camper at the world's darkest, most primitive campsite in the world any woman would find easy to use!

The Uncomforting Comforters

The beautification of my bedroom became a priority the day my sister went off to college and out of what was now considered "my bedroom." The plans I had were limitless and even though I had an operating budget of almost nothing, I was still in the planning stages of what would surely become the most beautiful bedroom on the face of the earth! In the years before my sister moved, I would anxiously wait for the new JCPenney catalog to arrive every spring and every fall. I would shuffle through to the back of that beautiful book where the comforter sets began and then, page by page I would slowly allow the splendor contained in those jaw dropping collections to ignite a fire in my designing eyes that would almost make me cry. To date I am almost 100% sure I never ordered anything from those catalogs, but it doesn't mean I didn't enjoy the escape I made from my sometimes colorless existence. I would imagine I lived in a house with 15 bedrooms and each one would be decorated in a completely different way.

Time passed and this love of a beautiful bedroom has never left me. The only problem I've encountered is the fact that men, (Don specifically) don't understand why there must be 8 to 10 pillows on a bed that are only there to enhance the beauty of the coordinating comforter! Before I moved in with Don I began "Bevitizing" the house just a bit when I stayed with him every other weekend. I decided a little change here and there would help him to adjust slowly, preparing him for the bigger changes that would eventually come. The first order of business that needed to be addressed will come as no shock to you. I was going to replace the black, gray, fuchsia, purple and aqua comforter that was on the bed. I thought about this first and decided that giving Don a new comforter for his birthday would make it seem less daunting. "Oh look, a present. Isn't this nice? You're going to absolutely love this handsome brown plaid micro mink comforter Don! It's so incredibly soft, here, feel!" The excitement for this new comforter was not transferring over to him like I had hoped. He simply said, "It looks hot. I don't like hot blankets. I guess we'll see." Now, he didn't appear to be excited but I'm pretty sure I didn't hear any doors slam shut in his head which meant he was willing to give it a try! I was more than satisfied with that and so I whipped it into place and when the time came we both got in bed and covered up and eventually drifted off to sleep. About three hours later I woke up to such intense heat I thought I was going to burst into flames! This comforter was so hot! It didn't seem to be bothering Don as he was still sleeping so I decided to just slide it ever so carefully off of me and hoped I would wake up before him so I could put it back on. He didn't need to know he was right, right? After having night one behind us I came up with a plan about an hour into night two. I told him my back was aching and headed out to the couch. He still didn't say anything. After three nights under the warmest comforter on the entire planet Don said, "You know Bev, this comforter is very nice but it's just too hot! It has to go!" I breathed a huge sigh of relief and informed my sweat glands they would finally have the night off!

I let a couple of months pass before revisiting the new comforter idea but eventually I found a lightweight set that appeared to offer the beauty so important to me and a bit less warmth for Don. It had matching shams and throw pillows and I decided to give it a whirl. Don wasn't terribly surprised to see my second attempt heading towards the bedroom and he was nice enough to not attempt to talk me out of trying again.

31

In the middle of the night I remember waking up as I was a bit chilly. I felt around to see if Don had pulled the comforter off of me and then he woke up and he was chilly and as he walked around the foot of the bed en route to the bathroom he realized why we were both cold. The comforter had slipped onto the floor. Apparently the smooth nylon fabric on the back side of this comforter made it just a bit too lightweight and very unpredictable. It played games with us the entire night before being fired on its first shift. It was sort of like furniture polish on a linoleum floor. If you don't know what I mean, please don't try it.

I'm here to say that I have officially given up on having a gorgeous bedroom ensemble because the soft ones are too warm, and the pretty ones won't stay on the bed. There's a small part of me that is thinking about making a patchwork quilt but I'm not 100% sure if I'm ready to see why all the seasoned quilters I've talked to had terrified looks on their faces when I told them I was thinking about making a king size quilt as my first project. I'll keep you posted!

The Fling

If you have a dog and you walk it in town, I'm pretty sure you've picked up some droppings at least once. I got in the habit of carrying two plastic bags with me when Missy, our 115-pound St. Bernard/Bloodhound cross and I would head out for our daily adventure. One bag was used to stretch over the hand that would be doing the picking up and one was for the prize the bagged hand was fetching. I'm not sure why I didn't invest in one of those state-of-the-art pooper scoopers. I suppose I didn't want to carry it on our lengthy 2-3-mile walks and the bag thing worked fine. If she did her business close to home, I would sit the bag on the edge of the road and pick it up when we passed by on our way back and if she did her business farther from home I would usually find a garbage can in the park to toss it in. I don't seem to have a problem with tossing. It's my flinging that needs work. Keep reading, you'll understand.

One day, just after leaving our yard and crossing the street, Missy decided it was already time to take care of her potty business. Once she was finished, I picked up her results and tied the bag handles in a knot and decided to fling it onto our driveway. I walked across the street and stood on the edge of our next-door neighbor's yard so I would be a bit closer to my targeted spot. There was only one small problem. I have flinging issues, but I don't often remember this until the object I'm flinging has left my hand. From past experience the biggest problem had something to do with the timing and when I should let go. Due to the fact that I didn't recall my past experiences soon enough, the bag was airborne......going straight up........and over.......and landed in the neighbor's beautiful pine tree! Now, this neighbor was very meticulous. I'm not so sure I didn't see him, on one or more occasion, vacuum his yard. He wanted it to look like he was vacuuming his car but how many people park their car on their front lawn to vacuum it? Very suspicious, don't you think? Everything was always perfect, everything, except......his neighbors! I tried to think quick and decided I had three options. I could ignore it, hope no one saw me fling it and walk away. I could go up to his door and explain what had happened or I could shake the ever-loving crap (literally) out of the branches and hopefully knock the bag down. I opted for the shake and thankfully it worked. This was clearly one of those moments you hoped no one was watching but it wasn't long before I was told there were indeed witnesses and they thanked me for the great laugh they got at my expense! It got even funnier when I was stupid enough to tell them what was in the bag!

Interrupted Travel Plans

Hindsight is really not as useful as foresight. I've had situations where foresight was trying desperately to make a connection with me but the override feature in my brain wouldn't let me respond in a way that would prevent certain circumstances. I remember one such incident with "certain circumstances" that I wish I could forget.

It was a hot and humid July afternoon. There were not a lot of kids my age in the tiny little town I grew up in but there were always a couple to hang out with and as my luck would have it, those two usually wanted to hang out with me at the same time. I became the mediator or the one "caught in the middle" when it came to these two particular friends of mine. They didn't click all that well, but I clicked with both of them and every once in a while, I would suggest we all hang out together. I remember one day in particular. Some of the details are fuzzy but the end result remains crystal clear unfortunately. I was at Jill's house and we decided to ride our bikes over to Stephanie's house. We raced outside to get on our two wheeled wonders and quickly realized I didn't have mine with me. Hmmm, now what? Jill said, "Why don't you ride my brother's bike. He's not home and as long as we put it back where we found it, he won't even know."

It seemed like a harmless plan. We would only be gone for a little while and he surely wouldn't have a clue we borrowed his bike if it was right where he left it when he got home. What could possibly go wrong, right?

We unanimously agreed and off we strolled, down the street to Stephanie's house. When we arrived, there were a couple of vehicles in the narrow driveway but still room for us to park our bikes. This is where foresight was attempting to establish a connection with my brain. I got off the bike and lowered the kickstand. I began to walk away but I heard a faint message coming from my brain. I believe it said "This is not a good spot for this bike. What if someone decides to back the car out of the driveway. They will run it o-v-e-r!" I know I heard these words but the thrill of playing Barbies and eating ice cream bars and drinking pop in the air-conditioned comfort of Stephanie's playroom stifled the soft-spoken logic coming from that place in my brain that was trying to keep Jill's brother from killing us. Before long we were planning a vacation to Hawaii for Barbie and packing her suitcase and driving her to the airport in her Barbie car to get on the Barbie airplane! Life was good......that is until our travel plans for Barbie were interrupted by someone yelling something down the stairs from the kitchen. Stephanie went to see what they were saying and upon her return to the Barbie International Airport she said, "Someone parked a bike behind the car and my sister just ran over it." You could have knocked me over with the feather from one of Barbie's hats! Life as I knew it and Jill knew it was over. O-V-E-R! If Stephanie's parents didn't kill us Jill's parents would and if they spared us my parents would kill us and if we talked them out of it, Jill's "bikeless" brother was surely going to kill us.

The dust eventually settled and frazzled nerves calmed down and once we decided Stephanie's parents weren't going to let her sister back over us, we went outside to have a look at the wreckage. It wasn't good. The wheels were no longer round. They were sort of shaped like jellybeans. The handlebars were flat and no matter what we tried; we couldn't make it look the same as it did when we took it out of Jill's yard. Quickly, I offered my dad's services. He was a blacksmith and he was able to repair almost anything! Unfortunately, we learned he could fix almost anything EXCEPT bikes that had been run over by stupid big sisters! I'm sure Jill's brother got a new bike. I'm not sure if my dad offered to pay for it but it might explain why my dad had such an enormous garden every year and probably why he would share his fresh organic produce with my friend's parents. I think I just figured out why he thought I should weed the mile-long row of green beans now too. This was torture because I didn't even like green beans! Dad was a smart man!

A "Stressed" Ball

My mother is and has always been a wonderful person. She was the most patient, loving mother an extremely shy kid that was afraid of everything could ever have. Some parents want their kids to move out by the time they're 18 but my mother convinced her little "Bubbles" that I should never feel there was a certain age I needed to be gone so I stuck around until I was in my mid-twenties. My decision to marry meant I had plans to move out of my parent's home. I did think about eloping and telling my mom I was at a slumber party, but I think she would have eventually figured out I wasn't telling her the truth. She didn't handle the "empty nest" syndrome very well and became very depressed when I flew the coop. Twenty years passed and I went through a divorce and found myself asking her if I could rent my old bedroom for a few months. She was more than happy to welcome me with open arms which was very nice. There was only one small problem. She shaved 30 years off my age and in her mind, I was now 17. When I was actually 17 the old saying "You can never go home." always bugged me. How sad. Why would anyone tell you that you can never go home? Who would ever leave if they believed this? When I was 47 I knew they meant "You will never want to go home because your mother will treat you like you're 17." She checked up on me. If I wasn't home from work by 6 pm she would drive by my workplace really slow checking to make sure I wasn't lying dead on the pavement out front. She would call me to see if I wanted my mail brought to the store and if she should keep supper warm and she washed my clothes. To some this might sound wonderful and for the most part, it was, and I did appreciate a lot of the sweet things she did, but our relationship wasn't the same as it was when I was her little girl. We had both changed. She liked the house 90 degrees in the winter and 60 degrees in the summer. I was closer to 68-72 degrees year round. I liked to unwind after work in the silence of my room because I talked to people all day long and she liked to visit. I wasn't a fan of having both the radio and television on at the same time, but she was. I knew this situation was temporary, so I did my best to cope with the everyday stress of living with my mother. One night I got up to use the bathroom and I went into the kitchen to get a drink of water before returning to bed. I saw a dark colored ball sitting near the sink. It looked like one of those stress balls I used to make by putting flour in a balloon. You could buy them too and I'm not so sure I didn't have a factory made one as well, but I have no idea where they ended up. They were so fun to squeeze, and I think they did actually relieve stress. Well, the dark colored ball near the sink sure looked like a stress ball to me and in my half-awake stupor I decided to give it a squeeze. I sort of wondered where mom would have gotten a stress ball, but

37

I reached over and gave it a nice tight squeeze and found out, it wasn't a stress ball. It was a purple plum. It sustained injuries. It did not recover. I went back to bed.

Note to self: Everything that glitters probably isn't gold and there's a good chance that round dark colored balls sitting on your 77 year old mother's kitchen counter are most likely there to relieve something but it probably isn't stress!

A Foot Sized Mouth

Have you ever had one of those moments when you say something totally innocent but the people around you burst into laughter because what you said can be taken in a completely different way than what was intended? I've had countless occasions of "foot in mouth" situations but there are two in particular, that have permanently attached themselves to my memory. I'm going to share them with you because I believe it's good to laugh at yourself once in a while and give others a reason to laugh too as long as it doesn't hurt anyone.

With that being said, here goes. The summer before last I had a customer come into the store where I worked on a regular basis and every day, beginning in May, he would dig out his tank tops and shorts. It was no big deal. Lots of people wear tank tops and shorts. I think he stood out more in my mind because he started early in the spring and wore them late into the fall. One day after the weather had started to get chilly, he walked in and that was the day he switched his wardrobe back to sweatshirts and jeans. I could have said nothing. That would have been for the best but the filter in my brain malfunctioned and like an idiot I yelled out, "Hey Don, I hardly recognize you with pants on!" The roar of laughter shook the ceiling tiles! I knew what I meant. He knew what I meant but everyone else thought something completely different!

I had a similar incident several years ago. This one transpired when I ordered supplies for my doll business. They were delivered by FedEx and would usually arrive around 11 am. I got in the habit of wearing my big, pink, floor length fleece robe most of the day if I had no plans to go out. It was not revealing in any way and I decided signing for my shipments while wearing it was perfectly fine. The delivery guy and I would occasionally joke about me still being in my pajamas, but it really was no big deal. Eventually I became a bit burned out from my stay-at-home doll business so I decided to go to work at a local factory as a temp and when I got the job, I was informed they would be using me whenever and wherever they needed help. One of my first jobs was to work as a receptionist in the marketing services building for a few days. I was surrounded by a lot of people I didn't know. They were coming and going and working in cubicles and no one was familiar until the FedEx guy walked in with a delivery. It was right about the time a bunch of people had gathered near the door for their morning break. I recognized him right away and he recognized me, and I said, "Hey, I know you! This is what I look like with clothes on!" Once again, I knew what I meant, and he knew what I meant but everyone else thought something completely different!

I suppose I could feel bad or embarrassed, but I'd rather laugh about it and celebrate these silly little tricks my mouth plays on me when I least expect it!

The Blue Rocket

The other day my mom headed out to get her mail. What she didn't know is just how exciting things were going to get when she least expected it. She has three children and due to the fact that none of us want to see anything bad happen, we are constantly reminding her to be careful. She likes to be as independent as she can possibly be and part of that involves going out to get her mail. Sometimes there will be an icy build up near her mailbox in the winter, so she keeps a bag of ice melt in the front seat of her car and when needed, she sprinkles the ice before getting out to get the mail. The other day she drove past the box a bit closer than usual, opened the door, got out, got the mail and then once back in the driver's seat, she shifted the car into reverse instead of drive, hit the accelerator and caught the door on the mail box stand. She was so terribly upset when this happened, she wasn't quite sure what to do. She drove ahead and found out the door wouldn't shut so she drove into the yard with the door open wide. She got out of the car and went inside to call my sister. My sister did her best to calm mom's frazzled nerves, but she was still upset. She called me a bit later and I could tell the frazzled nerves were still in intensive care so I did my best to calm her down, reassuring her that it would get fixed and that everyone has things like this happen. I realize this was very upsetting but listening to her account of what transpired put a "Howdy Doody" type smile on my face that will resurface for years to come. She said, "Bev, do accelerators make the car go faster in reverse than when they're in drive? I told her I wasn't really sure and then I asked why. She replied, "Everything happened so fast, but I do remember this, when I put my foot on that %$#& gas pedal, the car took off backwards like a rocket!"

I was very thankful she was not injured and that the damage will not require extensive repairs. During the phone call I was reassuring my sweet mother that this type of thing happens to a lot of people. On the inside, however, I was watching the video that formed in my brain as she was asking me questions about the "rocket" she had just driven into the yard with the door ajar and doing my best to stifle the laughter that was attempting a rather forceful entrance into the conversation.

A New Home For Bumper

I am an animal lover. I'm especially fond of cats and I'd do almost anything to bring joy and comfort to a cat that crosses my path.

A couple of years ago Don and I were staying with my mom for the weekend. The sun was going down, but it wasn't completely dark yet. Don was outside visiting with my brother and I came outside to join the conversation but before I got to where the guys were, I heard some very loud MEOWS off in the distance. I looked around and eventually saw a little black face across the highway peeking out between the tall grass. He was very verbal and for a fluent meow translator like myself, I knew exactly what he was saying. "I'm lost, I'm hungry, I can't find my mom and I'M AFRAID OF THE DARK!!!" I walked over to him and with a tiny bit of coaxing, he was my new friend. We bonded very quickly, and he started to purr, and I knew I had a situation on my paws...err, ah, I mean hands that would require some quick thinking. I knew I couldn't take him home as Don is terribly allergic to cats. I knew my mom wouldn't want him as she is not a cat lover and then I thought about my sister. They have a huge shed filled with bails that cats had come and gone from for years. It was sort of like a cat hotel. I just knew they wouldn't care if I took my new little vibrating fur ball there, so he and I piled into my car. If you've ever invited a cat to be a passenger in your car, you know how much they don't like it. He meowed and carried on and gave me all kinds of reasons about how happy I was that my sister only lived two miles away. During the drive I mapped out my plan. I knew I had to get the kitten in the shed. I knew I needed to shut the door and I knew I needed to get out of the yard before he saw me leave so he wouldn't try to follow me. By this time, it was pretty dark so I drove up as close to the shed as I possibly could and left my lights on so I could see inside. I carried my little friend into his new home and positioned him in front of the food dish and made my way out the door and slammed it shut. I hopped in my car and all of a sudden, I felt as if I was a stunt woman in an action adventure movie and I was overcome with the desire to whip my car around in a circle and peel out!!! In reality, I was running from a kitten. For a brief moment though, there was nothing about this plan that didn't make sense, that was until my bumper matched wits with the solid steel windmill I didn't see when I pulled in the yard. OUCH! The mark it left on my car was not pretty. The bumper sustained very noticeable injuries. I wasn't exactly sure why, but it appeared to have gotten caught on something. I didn't realize until the next day that my passenger side front tire actually rolled inside the wheel rim dad used as the base of this windmill when he built it. My sister had flowers planted in the rim and told me the ones with the tire tracks on them didn't survive but the ones that were still standing looked great. I tried to laugh but I had a terrible pit in my stomach because I realized my cat rescue was going to cost me $500. On the bright side, "Bumper" as my brother-in-law so affectionately named him, decided he liked his new home and became a very happy, well-adjusted adult cat.

I'm quite sure working for an insurance company that handles auto claims would never be boring provided everyone that reports accidents is as honest and as full of details as I am. At one point, during my conversation with my claim's person, they snorted while laughing out loud!

Tape, Paper Clips or Staples?

Wardrobe malfunctions are never fun. I've had several and all of them qualify for my "Most Embarrassing Moments" list. One that made my "Top Ten" list happened while I was working at the post office. There were three male mail carriers that sorted mail in the morning and then returned once they were finished with their routes to drop off the letters they had collected during the day. I was wearing a pair of black jeans and a longer yellow and white striped sweater with a black design embroidered on the front. I said it was longer but not one that covered my entire back end. (Knowing this will be important as you read on.) It was around 2 pm that I decided to go back and close the window that had gotten opened earlier due to the fact that one of the carriers was a bit too warm as he was sorting his share of the daily mail. I walked over and to this day, I'm still not sure what made me reach back and brush my hands across my back side as I approached that window but what I discovered sent shock waves that began at the top of my head and shot clean through to the tips of my toes! I had, at some point, blown the entire back seam out of my jeans! The worst part is, I had no idea when it happened so there was a chance, I had been working all day like this! Not only had

I worked with three guys, I had also waited on numerous customers that were given ample opportunities to know more about my underwear than they would have ever needed!

I had to come up with a plan. The first one wasn't good. I thought about racing out the door screaming that the office was on fire. That one would have gotten way too complicated and I knew I would be the one filling out the 3412-page report required when anything in the office went wrong. The second plan wasn't good either. I thought about asking the very next customer that walked in the door to assume my post until I returned. That would be the time when the Postmaster General just happened to be in town to pay this tiny little office a visit only to find out the employee responsible for rolling out the red carpet had actually gone home to change clothes in the middle of the day so I kept thinking. Maybe I could tape them together or maybe paper clip them back together or maybe, just maybe I could staple them back together! Yes! That will work so I seized the first opportunity when there were no customers at the window, and I grabbed the stapler and we backed into the bathroom to reconstruct my jeans. When I slipped them down to my knees I almost fell to my knees as it wasn't until then I saw that I was wearing my underwear with the big rainbow-colored polka dots on them!!! Really?! Why today? I knew I couldn't spend a lot of time thinking about how humiliated I was, but I did have to have a small meltdown before the "It's no big deal" feeling took effect. It appeared the staples would hold but only if I didn't exert any pressure on them so the staples, the jeans and I decided to stand for the rest of the day. We all knew sitting down would not be the thing to do and so I stood until 4:30, constantly yanking on my almost, but not quite long enough sweater. I worried a little bit about actually sitting down to drive home and how those staples might react when they're pushed beyond what we discussed in the bathroom but then I told myself, how bad could it hurt to have 25 tiny little staples open up? Everything would be fine. When I could finally leave the office, I got into my car and drove home. The pain was immediate. I was glad I had a 1.5 minute commute. I was glad the wind wasn't blowing and I was glad no one saw the smoke coming from our back yard when I broke a city ordinance by starting a fire that would allow me to torch the polka dot underwear and the jeans and the staples that left their marks in places I could feel better than I could see!

Differing Perspectives

There are always two sides to everything. A front and a back. A positive and a negative. An up and a down. A day and a night and a man that can't sleep and a woman that can. Each side has value and a completely different perspective, more often than not. With that being said, I have to share the rest of the story about the night, not long ago, when Don managed to snag approximately 30 minutes of sleep the whole night. My earlier story reported that he gave me a shake that caused me to wake up rather abruptly and head out to the couch. I'm sure you remember reading about my frustration when he chose to give me one of those "THE HOUSE IS ON FIRE!" nudges. Here's the part I didn't know anything about until last night.

On the night of the "abrupt awakening" supper was finished. The taped television shows were watched, and the time had finally arrived that Don began his nightly trip down the hall to greet the soft, cushy bed that waited patiently for his return each night. It almost always delivered a wonderful night's sleep to him, so he had no reason to believe otherwise. He slid underneath the cool, crisp sheets and wrapped himself in the comforts his tired aching body looked so forward to at day's end. I was still at work which would give him a little over an hour to slip into a restful sleep that would not be easily awakened by my presence.

Not long after Don hit the hay, I made my way in the door trying to be as quiet as I could be and as I inched my way down the hall, I listened for the tell-tale signs that Don was out. Due to the fact that I needed to unwind for a while before heading to bed, I slipped into the office and checked emails and read a few Facebook posts. Now that I think about it, I don't remember hearing any snoring that night which was not a good sign. Eventually the time came for me to shut down the computer and get some sleep. I brushed my teeth and crawled into bed. I heard some pillows getting punched, some frustrated sighs and perhaps a small amount of teeth gnashing which meant things weren't going all that well for my honey. It wasn't long before I fell asleep and the next thing I remembered was being shook and overtaken by fear that the house was on fire!

That was my perspective. Here is Don's.

Apparently, he couldn't get comfortable. His back was bothering him. He had been tossing and turning right up until I came to bed. This explains why I didn't hear him snoring peacefully when I tip toed down the hall earlier. He dozed off just long enough to unknowingly relinquish a portion of the bed he liked to call his side. According to him I had managed to find the middle of the bed and that is where I planted my snoring, roaring lifeless body. He gave me a gentle nudge hoping it would convince me to roll over. It didn't work so he tried the nudge tactic approximately 20 more times and emitted a low-pitched growl followed by some involuntary teeth gnashing between each try. He didn't think the growl and teeth gnashing helped at all but apparently it happened automatically. He said the only response his gentle nudges were getting was a groan and a couple lip smacks and then the snoring would start all over again! He did a quick measure of the amount of bed on his side of me versus my side of me and decided there were roughly two more inches of bed on my side. Getting comfortable just wasn't happening and upon his return from the bathroom he thought about trying the deluxe and much wider side of the bed I wasn't using. He was so bored at one point he thought about getting the tape measure out just to see how accurate he was about the space on my side being two inches wider. He told me he's decided not to have the feather pillows fluffed and cleaned as they had quite a workout and were seemingly quite rejuvenated. He also explained that when he delivered the shake that woke me up, he was wiped out and dangerously close to that place we refer to as " His Wit's End."

Monday morning finally arrived, and it wasn't at all surprised to see just how miserable Don was. Mondays like to see people this way. It reinstates their credentials. Mondays would never want it getting around that someone actually liked them and there was no danger of that happening on Don's account. As for me, I heard him leave for work and it was then, I got off the couch I had stomped down the hall to curl up on earlier, headed back down the hall in the opposite direction and enjoyed the soft, cushy bed complete with pillows that required absolutely no fluffing thanks to Mr. Wit's End!

A Solution With A Glitch

For those of you that have an ample amount of flesh between your thighs, the following information will be incredibly easy to understand and possibly benefit you in some way.

When my new job began at the first fabric store I worked for, I was told I could wear pants during the week, but dresses were mandatory on weekends. I wasn't terribly thrilled about this idea as I had a bit of a problem when I wore pantyhose and I would never think of wearing a dress without them. My thighs have always been very good friends. They've been next to each other for years and they tend to rub together when I walk. There are people that don't have this problem, but I've seen a lot of people that do and I'm thinking you will completely understand my dilemma provided you, yourself, have worn panty hose with your dresses.

I haven't researched this yet but I'm betting a man invented pantyhose. A woman would never invent something that would make other women so miserable. They're constructed from fabric created when elastic, almost microscopic threads are knitted, forming what appears to be something you will never fit into no matter how hard you try but the magical elasticity of them actually allows miracles to happen right before your very eyes. Putting on a pair of these wonderful creations is sort of like putting the water back in the grape when it has already been classified as a raisin. We learn at an early age to scrunch the entire leg of the nylon up into our hand, stretch it over our toes and then slowly pull the remainder of the nylon up until our leg is completely transformed into this beautiful, smooth and newly colored appendage. We repeat this step for the other leg and then pull the body of the nylons up to our bras if you wear the size I wear. I haven't tried this but on some of mine I'll bet I could cut a hole on each side and bring them up over my shoulders, but I'll save that discovery for another chapter.

Once they're on, they're a part of you. They don't feel bad at first but after several hours they have a tendency to turn on you if you are one of those people with ample thighs. The skin is forced through the holes like a piece of cheese through a grater and as the thighs rub together, tiny pieces of skin get sanded away. Over time this causes extreme pain. An 8-hour shift at the fabric store falls into the "extreme pain" category. I knew I would have to come up with a solution but "forgetting" to wear a dress every weekend was only going to work for a short time. There had to be yet another solution but what would it be?

I decided to cut a piece of tricot from one of my older slips. I made it long enough so that I could slide one side down one leg of my hose and one side down the other leg of my hose before I pulled them up all the way hoping it would protect my inner thighs from any further torture. Much to my amazement, it worked! I was so happy I had finally found a solution to my very painful problem. It just worked and worked and worked every time I wore a dress!

It seems that with every new invention, however, there are glitches. I remember the day quite well when my tricot leg liner glitch arrived. It was mid-afternoon on a Saturday. I was wearing a royal blue blouse and a white pencil skirt. The skirt was so cute. It was sort of short and it had a slit in the back and at the top of the slit was a bow I made from the same material. I was standing at the frame shop counter with my back to the cutting table and one of my fellow employees walked up and said under her breath, "Bev, I think you have a piece of toilet paper stuck inside the leg of your pantyhose. You might want to run to the bathroom and get that taken care of." Immediately I was mortified. I knew exactly what had crawled out of one leg and into the other! I remember my trip to the bathroom, and I remember getting everything put back where it belonged, and I'll never forget just how much I still hate wearing pantyhose! I'm sure my thicker thigh sidekicks will completely understand!

The Cherry Bandits

Cherries are one of my favorite fruits and cherry is always the flavor I will choose when it comes to hard candy, taffy, ice cream topping or tootsie pops! I love, love, love cherries! I love them so much that I will stop at almost nothing to get some......almost.

Every week my friend and I would drive 27 miles to attend our Weight Watchers meeting. After the meeting was over and our minds were filled with nutritious ideas, we would head to the grocery store to see what exciting things we could add to our healthy menu so that we could enjoy waving goodbye to yet another pound or two the following week.

On one particular occasion we walked in the door of the store and were greeted by the most beautiful cherries we had ever seen! Gigantic, burgundy, shiny and perfect were all words that could be used to describe what we saw. We both loved cherries and they're Weight Watcher friendly so before we knew it, we had several bags in each of our carts at the beginning of our grocery shopping adventure. We both needed a few other items but eventually we met up and were lucky enough to each get in a line that had no others before us and we both paid for our cherries at approximately the same time and then we both headed out to the

50

door. Once we began to load our purchases into the back seat, we noticed something very odd. Not only were we both frantically rummaging through our bags for our receipts but we both had rather funny looks on our faces. It didn't take long to realize her cherries came to around $48.00 and my cherry tally was nearly $39.00! We were in a bit of shock and hashed over what we thought our husbands would say when they found out what we had just paid for a few bags of cherries. It wasn't long and we were both laughing hysterically and wiping tears from our eyes!

We talked about keeping them and throwing our receipts away but being the honest women we both were, we knew we'd end up telling these guys how much we spent and feared we might both be wearing straight jackets awaiting our one-way trip to the loony bin! It was then I came up with a plan. Let's return them! We have our receipts! This is something I had never done with food before but there's a first time for everything. We piled out of the van and headed back to the store. We made a quick trip past the cherry area hoping to get some sort of grip on our overwhelming bouts of laughter and we actually saw the price clearly marked for all the cherry lovers to see.... except for maybe two!

Vacuum Vomit

I pity the souls that find everyday life boring. There are so many people that waste away their existence waiting for "their ship to come in" or leave Barbie dolls in boxes so they'll be worth more in maybe 300 years or save the good dishes for the company that shows up once every 365 days. I learned long ago that I would never survive as part of this group. After Christmas I take all of the gifts I receive out of the boxes and start letting these new things become a part of our daily life. I don't freak out when the tablecloth gets a spot on it. I don't panic if my whites aren't perfectly white and I really don't spend a lot of time trying to figure out how to remove soap scum from the shower walls. We like our home to be presentable and neat but definitely not sterile and perfect.

Due to the fact it was barber shop night at our house tonight, I knew the vacuum would be making an appearance once everything was "cut and dried." The routine is usually quite similar each time the barber shop opens. I arm myself with a scissors and a comb. Don whips a towel around his shoulders and waits patiently while I lower his ears. I remove the towel and step outside to give it a shake before tossing it in the washer and then one of us backs the vacuum out of its garage and before long the spare hairs are wistfully sucked into this incredibly hungry device. The barber shop whips its hypothetical closed sign into the spot made especially for it in the imaginary window, we flick the switch on the swirling barber pole out front and life continues on which usually involves some television watching or showering. Tonight was just a tad bit different.

We bought a new vacuum several weeks ago and although I assembled it, I couldn't remember just exactly how to remove the large clear plastic tube that traps the dirt. When I started the vacuum, I remembered thinking I should have dumped it the last time I used it but didn't so I decided I should do it now. I saw two release buttons and pushed them both, but nothing happened. At that moment Don arrived on the scene and saw yet another button and pushed it and POOOOOOFFFFF!!!! It was the right one but due to the fact that I had pushed the wrong two first meant the entire contents of the vacuum made immediate plans to empty itself on itself rather than wait until it was suspended over the garbage can. I am here to tell you, that vacuum holds A LOT OF DIRT!!! It was everywhere. It was in the air and up our noses......ah..ahhhh....ahhhhh....CHOOOOO!!! and all over the legs of the chairs, on us, on the vacuum and all over the floor. I grabbed the electric broom out of the closet, and I can honestly say this was the very first time I had ever vacuumed a vacuum! Once we had everything put back together Don took the newly emptied vacuum across the floor and before long, everything was looking good and I said to him, "It's kind of like the vacuum is cleaning up its own vomit." The best thing about the whole incident is that we both laughed, we worked on the solution together, we made a memory and isn't that what life is all about?

Chocolate Pudding & TP

When my big sister got married and started having babies, I was just about the happiest aunt there could ever be! I loved to spoil my nieces and let them eat chocolate cake for breakfast when they stayed with me and break all the rules moms and dads create for their children to live by.

One day my sister asked me to go shopping with her and my two adorable nieces. At the time Andrea was around 3 years old and Allison was old enough to sit upright in a highchair without towels packed around her but little enough to be scary and incredibly unpredictable. We let Allison decide when we were all getting hungry due to the fact that she was the most unstable if anything went wrong. To a baby, an empty stomach ranks very high on the "something is terribly wrong" list and when she cried, everyone knew there was a problem. My sister decided we should eat at a buffet type restaurant. She liked those due to the fact that it was easy to find things Allison could eat. Allison was an adorable baby but she could turn on you in a flash and be screaming bloody murder for no apparent reason. There were many times I was so glad she wasn't mine when she was a baby. I was the aunt. I had the option of tossing her into her mother's arms and when I did, I would RUN!

We ended up having a rather nice lunch experience that day at the buffet restaurant meaning Allison held off screaming until we had all finished our food and it was then that Andrea announced she had to go potty. Becky glanced my direction and I knew that look on her face. It was that, "Which one do you want?" look. I knew taking Andrea to the bathroom would be much easier than trying to calm Allison, so they headed to the car and I was on my way to the bathroom with the quiet, well-mannered potty trained one that wasn't crying. I sort of forgot that Becky put her elbow in Andrea's bowl of chocolate pudding when she was getting up from the table, but it made us laugh and it was no big deal. Andrea got some on herself too but what harm could a little pudding do?

When Andrea and I got to the bathroom I lined the toilet seat with long strips of toilet paper. I had gone through my sister's rigorous training program on how to keep her kids as germ free as possible, so I knew I had to do this. Once it was covered, I picked Andrea up and put her on the seat. She was quite little, so she gripped the toilet with her cute little hands. What I didn't know is that her cute little hands were wearing some of that incredibly sticky chocolate pudding. I think my sister did mention something about making sure to wash Andrea's hands, but I was sure she meant after tinkling. Before long Andrea was ready to be lifted off the toilet and those long strips of toilet paper came with her. It was then that I remembered the chocolate pudding and I was quite impressed at how well it worked to glue the toilet paper to Andrea's hands. I gave them a tug and thought I got them all in the toilet and we headed to the sink to wash off the pudding and the tiny bits of toilet paper that came with us when we left the stall.

Finally it was time to head out to the car and for some reason, I was walking ahead of Andrea and what I didn't know is that one of those longs strips of toilet paper we had used to line the seat had attached itself to my shoe without me realizing it. Andrea was making an attempt to help me out, but she was just far enough back so that every time she reached down to grab that sticky streamer, I would take another step. Apparently, this happened quite a ways back as I began to notice people looking at me. It was then I glanced back and realized what was going on! By this time I was right next to the salad bar and all I could think was, "I've got to get rid of this!" so I grasped the opportunity and the edge of the salad bar, unloaded my newly acquired shoe attachment and Andrea and I went bursting out the door.

It was much later in the day when I regained my composure. It wasn't until then that I was able to tell Becky what all the hysterical laughter was about. I'm sure everyone has had toilet paper streamers attached to their shoes while traipsing through an incredibly busy restaurant, right? It's really not a big deal, really it isn't.... unless of course, it's happening to you!

A Magic Cooking Wand

Multitasking is something a lot of us do. It seems that we feel the need to convince our hands and our brains that it is, in fact, possible to do more than one thing at a time. I've been guilty of surfing the internet while making an attempt at an intelligent conversation on the phone. It sort of works but have you ever asked someone a question and as the words are coming out of your mouth you sort of remember asking that very same question and feel quite sure you received an answer? Perhaps you've been half listening to the person on the other end of the line and then all of a sudden there's dead silence. You know they've asked your opinion on something but because your brain wasn't fully engaged in what was being said you stumble and stammer and make a feeble attempt to change the subject. I hate to admit I'm guilty, but there have been a few times when I was distracted and convinced myself I was capable of giving 100% of my attention to two completely different things at the same time. Not all multitasking is the same. I have been successful folding the laundry, making the bed, organizing my desk, washing the dishes and baking while on the phone and the only glitch I remember is accidentally dropping the phone in my dish water and then I guess there was that time when I was making zucchini bread.....

Late last fall Don brought home two huge zucchinis from a friend's garden. I really don't like to bake but if encouraged, I will eventually give in. A few days before the zucchini would have been ready to toss in the garbage, I decided I should probably whip up something, so I found a couple of different recipes I wanted to try. I picked up some cute little foil pans and decided to make 8 cute little loaves of zucchini bread. I will sometimes buy things like cute little pans in an attempt to convince myself I don't hate baking. With 8 loaves, Don and I would each be able to take some to work and I could easily freeze the others and take one out when we began to crave a little treat. I assembled all of the necessary tools and ingredients and got things going. About then, the phone rang. It was my mom. She had all kinds of things to tell me and before I knew it, I had the batter evenly distributed between the 8 pans and they were ready to pop in the oven. Just as I flipped the oven door open, I realized I had forgotten to spray the pans with non-stick cooking spray. I knew I didn't want to take a chance on the bread not sticking after going to all the work of peeling and grating a zucchini the size of a watermelon, so I scraped all the batter back into the bowl. I washed and dried the pans and sat them on the counter. (This is the part where talking on the phone and baking will probably have to be taken off my multitasking ability list.) I grabbed the bowl and once again I divided the batter evenly between the 8 cute little pans. They weren't looking nearly as cute as they originally did but they were still cute.

Mom was chattering away, and I was attempting to be a part of the conversation and get my bread baking but just as I opened the oven I realized I had forgotten to spray the pans AGAIN!!!!!! When something like this happens you experience a moment of disbelief. It's a moment when your eyes bulge out of your head and you say things to yourself you wouldn't normally say and then there's a bit of frustration followed by that "I could just cry" feeling. You entertain thoughts of fairy godmothers being real and you just know yours is going to appear and wave her glorious "magic cooking wand" over your bread in an effort to convince you there really are happily ever afters.

In reality, I dumped the batter back in the bowl again. I washed and dried those ridiculous little pans again and fought the urge to smash all 8 of them with a hammer. Don saw 8 delicious little loaves of zucchini bread sitting on the counter when he got home from work and said, "Hey, great, you used the zucchini. Now, that wasn't so bad, was it?" I didn't bite him but there may have been a low-pitched growl and a bit of teeth gnashing going on....just saying.

"The Chocolate Incident"

There's nothing more frustrating than thinking you have all the ingredients for something you plan to make only to discover, after a thorough investigation, that one of the key ingredients is missing! What you are about to read transpired out of my desire to create a 9 x 13-inch pan of the moistest, fudgiest unfrosted brownies in the world and the eminent danger the much needed chocolate chips were in.

Years ago I was married to a chocoholic. I tried to keep those adorable little fun size candy bars well stocked but when the day to replenish the stash inched closer, I should have known the chocolate chips weren't safe. I never came to the conclusion I should be hiding them or perhaps find a less likely place for them like the oven drawer or under the sink or maybe even out in the trunk of my car, so I suppose part of what happened was actually my fault. As a matter of fact, I even remember telling the chocoholic I planned to whip up a pan of Dump Bars the following day, so he knew there was, indeed, chocolate, somewhere. That was a huge mistake.

Some time passed and I got distracted folding some laundry and as I was heading to the bathroom to put the towels away, I ran across Christopher Columbus just after he made his discovery! The chocoholic was standing in the kitchen, the cupboard door was open hiding his face and I said, "What are you doing? You're not eating the chocolate chips, are you?" At first, I heard the rustling of plastic and an arm reaching into the cupboard followed by a very unconvincing "No." I walked over to him and removed the open bag of chocolate chips from the shelf they had just been slid onto. I walked over to the drawer and pulled out the scotch tape. I placed a small piece across the very small "4 chips at a time" size hole the bag was baring, and I said, "I'm hiding these!"

Unfortunately the house wasn't that big and making an attempt to hide something at that particular moment was quite ridiculous. The chocoholic followed my every move and due to the fact it was nearly time for bed I took them with me into the bedroom and crawled under the covers and waited for him to retreat. I didn't plan on falling asleep but the next thing I knew, it was morning and you can imagine my surprise when I woke up wondering what the lump was that was fighting for the same spot on the mattress as my ribs. I rolled over and saw the bag of chocolate chips. Well, I thought to myself, I guess I kept them safe from the chocoholic after-all!

I had to chuckle and when I picked them up, however, as I realized they were no longer chocolate "chips." During the night I unknowingly rolled on top of them and the nice warm body blanket they were covered with melted them completely and turned them into a solid bar of chocolate! My mission to save the chocolate chips failed miserably. The end result yielded one candy bar back in the stash and zero chocolate chips to dump on the dump bars! I've decided to include the recipe for these incredibly easy and delicious brownies. You can actually make them without chocolate chips. I learned this part the hard way, just saying!

Dump Bars

Dump 2 cups sugar, 5 eggs, 1 cup vegetable oil and 1 teaspoon of vanilla into a bowl and stir until well blended. Add 1 1/3 cups flour, 1/2 cup cocoa and 1 teaspoon salt and mix just until all dry ingredients are moistened. Dump the batter into a 9x13 pan that has been sprayed with non-stick cooking spray or call upon your fairy godmother and ask her to bring her non-stick cooking wand. (In order for that to make sense you might want to read my "Magic Cooking Wand" first.) Sprinkle the batter with chocolate chips or get creative and use 2 or 3 different kinds of chips. Bake at 350 degrees for 30-35 minutes or until the brownies begin to pull away from the sides of the pan. Cool and enjoy! I guarantee your chocoholic will absolutely LOVE these easy treats even if the chunks of chocolate you dump on them no longer resemble perfectly formed little drops!

A "Dad Style" Hug

My dad was not the kind and loving type. I have no memories of his arms open wide, waiting for a hug from his little girl. I don't remember being comforted when nothing seemed to be going my way. I don't ever remember him saying he was proud of me; I don't remember ever seeing "Dad" signed by him in a birthday card and I could have almost said he never told me he loved me but he managed to fit that in just before he died. This is probably sounding like a very sad story coming from a somewhat bitter daughter but if you continue reading, you might see it quite differently.

Dad married a woman that would allow him to "be the boss." They grew up in that generation where men were men that worked hard to provide for their families and the women took care of the children and the home. Together my parents brought a daughter and a son and then another daughter into the world and created a foundation for these 3 children that would prepare all of us for this crazy world we attempt to understand.

We didn't have money. I know this now but when I was a kid, I had no idea my friend's dads had better jobs with better pay and I'm pretty sure they didn't know that either. Dad provided us with a swing set, a sand box, a teeter totter he made and a tire swing. We all had bikes he picked up at auction sales. We swam in a dented old watering tank he most likely got from a farmer that had replaced it due to the fact it was damaged. Dad could always fix things and find a way to put them into our world. We probably didn't realize it then, but now we know he was actually "hugging" us and telling us he "loved" us the only way he knew how and sometimes that meant pounding the dents out of an old watering tank so his kids would have a place to cool off on those hot summer days when we weren't riding our bikes or making mud pies.

I didn't get to be a Girl Scout or take piano lessons or join 4-H or play in the school band, but I didn't know it was because my parents couldn't afford it. It was never something offered to us and we never questioned it. I didn't get an allowance. I got a job. I believe it was when I was in the 3rd grade, my dad would bring home the mail for an elderly lady that lived down the bumpy road and through a hole in the lilac bushes. I would deliver that mail to her doorstep, and she would pay me $2 a week. Our parents never took any of our money and they never forced us to save it. They let us decide what needed to happen and spending it was always at the top of my list. One of my first purchases was a mood ring I discovered at the tiny little grocery and variety store I shopped at on a regular basis. The ring was $6 but the lady that ran the store was willing to take payments. It took me 3 weeks to own that ring but what a valuable life lesson that taught me. Eventually I moved on to bigger and better things and before long I was the proud new owner of a digital clock radio! Now, not only did I know when I was happy, sad or angry but I also knew what time all of these emotions were taking place!

My parents never established a certain bedtime for us. Dad would say it was up to us just how tired we wanted to be in the morning. That took a while to click but he knew what he was doing, and he knew he wouldn't be the one to suffer if we didn't get enough sleep. If we woke up tired and cranky we knew better than to let him know as there was no place in his world for whining or tantrums. Mom was a bit more lenient with some of those things, but we knew better than to take advantage of that too often as we needed her to tell dad when we broke something. It always appeared less scary that way, at least for us.

As the years came and went, I eventually got married and moved out of my parents' home. My dad continued to shop at auction sales retrieving secondhand treasures and nothing gave him more pleasure than when he bought something he knew one of us was going to have a use for. One time he ran across an old doll he thought I would like, and he bought it for me. It was missing an arm, but he was sure I could fix it up. I mentioned earlier that he never told me he was proud of me, but he knew a doll missing an arm was surely in the right hands when it found mine.

Dad wasn't the kind and loving type but I'm beginning to realize just how blessed I was then, with a dad that always provided a safe and comfortable home for his wife and all of his children. I learned to respect people. I learned the value of a dollar and I learned that hugs and kisses can come disguised in ways only a grown child might understand.

My dad has been gone since May of 2009 but every once in a while he makes his presence known as I have a brother that is a lot like him. He's short tempered and he still picks on me and I'm pretty sure he's never hugged me. Last night while Don and I were sitting at the table playing cards, I heard my phone chirp to let me know I had received a text. It was from my brother. He had gone to a secondhand shop in search of something and ended up buying an old vintage doll buggy. He asked me what I thought it was worth as I've been in the doll business for nearly 20 years and I said I would do some research and get back to him. His next text read, "It's yours." It had never happened before in all my 49 years but last night, I got a "hug" from my brother, a "dad style" hug!

There's Always A Butt

I was working tonight with a wonderful young gal. She's very pleasant and upbeat. She does her best to accommodate our customers butt....there's always a butt, isn't there? She has a habit of leaning over the counter when she's jotting down numbers and leaning over the counter when she's cutting fabric and leaning over the counter when she's rolling remnants and tonight the moon was almost more than I could handle! It was a crescent moon and due to the fact that I saw it one too many times out of the corner of my eye I would have to say it was at least 9 inches by 18 inches and there was a whole lot more crack there than I wanted to see! Most people would probably just let it go but as I approach 50 I believe menopause may be moving in a few things. It's not completely unpacked but I do think it has made its mind up about settling in sometime soon and I'm almost positive it is what made me say, "You've got a whole lotta moon going on there tonight!" I wanted to just go up to her and take a hold of those low riding britches and hike 'em up but we have a lot of cameras and I didn't want the people that watch our every move to choke on their skittles.

Perhaps I'm a bit too modest but our mother had ways of letting us know that too much bare skin was inappropriate and for some reason, my sister and I are still both very careful about the skin we're willing to show. She has started to wear tank tops. She's such a rebel! (She'll love that line!) I'm not there yet but mainly because I hate my fat arms. I've started wearing tops cut a tiny bit lower than the turtleneck level I'm quite fond of and we're both willing to sport a rather nice assortment of capris in the summer. I realize some people are just incredibly comfortable in their own skin and I sort of wish I was a little more comfortable than I am, but never, ever, ever will you see a 9 x 18 crescent moon shining brightly on my back side!

I've been standing on my soap box quite a bit lately and the crowd that gathers usually laughs at me, but I do have valid points and there are just some things menopause won't allow me to overlook. I don't think anyone with 20/100 vision or worse could have missed that moon tonight. I've never exposed my buns in public and I always wonder about the people that do. Can they not feel a draft? Do they not care? Did they not have a mother that taught them what skin was appropriate to reveal and what skin wasn't? I am here to tell you; I know where my pants and all other parts of my outfit are almost all of the time. (There was that one exception I refer to in my chapter entitled "The Dressing Gamble" but I flick the switch now or lay things out the night before which has helped tremendously.) Years ago when I was in high school, our biology teacher put a parka on the skeleton in the science lab with a sign that said, "I'm modest." I didn't know what modest meant at the time but if I had I would have patted those bones on the back and said, "I completely understand!"

The Good Old Rainbow Tumblers

When I was little we would sit in the living room, as a family, every Sunday night and watch Mutual of Omaha's Wild Kingdom followed by Walt Disney. Sometimes dad would stop at the little beer joint in town and bring home an assortment of some of the most disgusting, readymade sandwiches ever created. They couldn't have been wrapped in airtight packaging as they always tasted like cigarette smoke. All mom needed to do was slide them onto a cookie sheet and pop them in the oven to warm them up and before we knew it, supper was ready. She would always pick up a six pack of those large returnable quart bottles of pop when she did her weekly grocery shopping and treat us to pop with our supper on the weekends. It was so exciting. She would get out the rainbow colored Tupperware tumblers and fill each one with some ice cubes and some bubbly, delicious, very much anticipated pop. It kind of made the sandwiches a bit more palatable and before we knew it, the sandwiches and pop were gone and our eyes were glued to the television set watching the best choice of shows between the 2 and 1/2 channels we had. When I say 2 and 1/2 channels I mean CBS, NBC and then half the time public broadcasting would come in but only if the wind wasn't out of the west and it wasn't cloudy.

When my pop had washed down the last bite of my sandwich I continued to hold the glass up to my mouth and found that if I sucked all the air out of it, it would stay on my face like magic! This was so cool. My brother and sister took turns grabbing onto it and pulling it off so each time I put it back on, I would suck even more air out of it. There was a kind of tingly feeling that I enjoyed so I kept doing it for quite some time. Eventually it was time to head upstairs for bed which meant fighting to see who got to use the bathroom first. I'm not sure what place I came in that night, but I do remember getting off the toilet and tossing a glance at myself in the mirror above the sink and something immediately caught my attention which prompted my brain to take another look.

O-H M-Y G-O-S-H!!!!!! WHAT'S WRONG WITH MY FACE???? I had a reddish ring all the way around my mouth that reached down to the bottom of my chin!!! Immediately, I was terrified! My heart began to pound, and my palms got clammy and I recruited my sister to examine the situation. It wasn't long before she was ready to deliver her diagnosis. She could tell I was hanging on her every word as I was sure I had only days left to live. At this point, I'm doubting I'll ever forget the words that came out of her mouth. It was like one of those scenes from a movie when everything begins to happen in s-l-o-w m-o-t-i-o-n. She said, "You gave yourself a hickie with that stupid Tupperware glass!" The wave of relief that swept over my body was amazing! I knew, at the very second my very intelligent and most observant big sister delivered my fate, she was indeed, right as right can be!

This story may be an interesting angle for the Tupperware company to use in their advertising. For years they've promoted their extraordinary seals and the freshness locked inside their "burped bowls" but not once have they said anything about the tremendous seal their glasses have when sucked to a person's face! Heck, I didn't need a boyfriend to give me hickies when I became a teenager. We had a set of rainbow tumblers!

Setting The Record Straight

I was a pretty good kid. When I think back to the few times I got in trouble or made a bad decision, there is one particular friend that comes to mind. It's probably best if I don't mention her name because she might end up reading this and plot my untimely death but then again, she might laugh and give me a call. Hearing her voice is something that hasn't happened in nearly 16 years and perhaps that is what inspired this post. I really, really miss her.

She and I met before kindergarten. She came over to my house with her suitcase full of Barbies and we headed up to my room to play. After our first meeting we knew we would be friends for life and over the course of our childhood years we made great use of our time together. We played Barbies and made mud pies and rode our bikes and blew bubbles and played hopscotch. There was never a dull moment when we were together. One day I called to see if she could come over and play. She asked me to hold on while she checked with her mom. I waited and waited and waited and began to wonder why she hadn't returned to the phone to tell me what her mom said and then I happened to glance out the dining room window and saw her walking up the sidewalk. So she was a little dingy, who cares. I liked her. She had cool barbies!

Eventually the freedom we experienced as toddlers and whatever that phase is in between being a toddler and a kindergarten kid came to an end and we were in school. I was no longer a baby. I had to start growing up. A lot of my childhood experiences are a bit fuzzy but then there are a few that have stayed with me. They had reasons for staying crystal clear. If you make it to the end, you'll see why.

It's not often you hear about a first grade kid fainting, but my friend literally fainted one day. She accidentally shut her fingers in her desk and apparently her pain threshold was clocking in at a negative thirty five that day and all of a sudden, there she was, on the floor, in a pile. Who would think first grade kids in the early 70's would get exposed to that kind of drama? I should have probably realized this was a sign and that I should stay as far away from her as possible but I liked her and you stick by your friends even if they have a pain threshold of a negative thirty five from time to time.

We spent a lot of time together so not having an issue that had consequences until we were 8 years old is actually pretty impressive. The following information is the first incident with this friend and it took place when we were in the 3rd grade. We knew we were supposed to be quiet but for some reason my friend said, "Pssst, Bev, I have something to tell you." I had no idea what she needed to tell me and wondered, for about a half a second, why it couldn't wait until recess. When you're 8 years old though, you don't have a fully functional, intricately wired "cause and effect" process installed in your brain so I leaned over to hear her breaking news. Several seconds into the story I felt some rather intense pain stemming somewhere near my left ear. It was Mrs. Matheny pulling me back to an upright position in my little desk. I got "Psssted" and asked to lean over but by leaning over I was the one that got in trouble. My friend was just lucky we had different desks in 3rd grade or we may have tested her pain threshold that day when no one was looking, just saying.

The next bout of trouble arrived in 5th grade. That same "friend" had gotten terribly sick causing her to miss a week of school. She was behind in several subjects and asked me if I would let her copy my math papers. I knew it wasn't a good idea and I remember my cousin saying, "Don't do it Bev. You're going to get yourself in trouble." I knew she was right but I was a bit of a pushover and I caved but I told my friend, "Whatever you do, don't let the teacher find these" as I slipped her the answers she needed, to get on top of her math homework. She told me not to worry and the next thing I knew, the school day was drawing to a close and the teacher announced that she needed my friend and me to stay after class. Lightning bolts shot through my body as I knew the reason had to be something bad. I was right. My friend accidentally let the teacher see my math papers and it landed me a punishment that not only exhausted my mind and my attention span but the lead in two pencils as well! I was instructed to write, "I will never give my math answers to anyone again." 150 times!!!!

Things rolled along pretty smooth for the next five years until the need for creativity arrived and this friend called upon me to help her out. The best part of this experience is the fact that we didn't get in any sort of trouble which was nice but what happened did sort of bug me and I have finally decided to set the record straight! Our English teacher asked us to rewrite a Christmas carol using some of our own words. I have no idea what song I chose for myself but I got the assignment done and probably got a good grade on it but no bells and whistles and no laughter came with my submission. I do remember, however, that I chose to rewrite "Frosty The Snowman" for my dear friend because she couldn't think of anything and desperately needed my help. The teacher loved "her" rewrite and sang it in front of the class and laughed like there was no tomorrow every time she got to the part that read...."and two eyes made out of raisins." It probably wasn't that funny but it sounded funny because it didn't flow with any of the other words and that's why I chose it. It wasn't predictable or anything near what the singer was expecting and that's what brought the laughs. Did my friend fess up and say, "I can't take all the credit for this because Bev helped me."? No, she didn't. She took all the credit. Well now, if you were there and you remember those "raisin eyes" you can thank me for that laugh because I wrote those words!

I've always tried to be a good friend but it isn't always easy. The same friend that talked me into rewriting her Christmas song also talked me into taking Shorthand rather than Home Economics our junior year. I'm not sure why I let her do this as I knew I would probably never use what I learned in Shorthand ever again once the class was over and I was right. I also knew what was going to be covered in Home Economics that year and how incredibly valuable it would have been to me as an adult but I wanted to make my friend happy so I let her persuade me to take Shorthand. I'm not sure why I let her do things like that to me. Saying no just wasn't something that was easy for me to do. Perhaps there will be a young person that ends up reading this post and maybe it will help them to understand, sometimes friends will do their darnedest to talk you into doing things you really don't want to do and it is okay to say no. I sort of wish I had figured out how to do that a few times but the view looking back is always a whole lot clearer.

In reality and without anger I can honestly say giving in to this friend all those years ago shaped a very important part of what makes me who I am. Had I decided not to be friends anymore with someone that faints I would have said no to the compassion taking root in my heart. The ear being pulled taught me to respect authority. The sentence writing solidified the teacher's desire to see all of her students succeed by doing their own homework. The extra bit of song writing I didn't get credit for forged a very necessary amount of humility within me that has come in handy numerous times since then and by taking Shorthand I established a friendship with my teacher that has gone on for years in my adult life. Isn't insight an amazing thing? I suppose I wouldn't have nearly as much had I said no more often in those incredibly crystal clear formative years!

Phones, Balloons & Respect

I found out yesterday that if I enter our home phone number and Don's work number into my phone and hit send, my phone thinks I'm trying to reach someone in Russia! I have a new cell phone and I'm still getting used to it and for some reason it doesn't always get rid of the first number I enter even after I have made the call, so when I dial the next number, my phone dials both! I figured this out yesterday. I had called our house and then Don's shop and I heard my phone saying something about international charges and when I pulled it away from my ear, I saw Russia blazing across my screen! I fumbled around and hit the "end" button a bunch of times and it finally stopped trying to pry that unsuspecting Russian citizen off their couch.

A while back I remember reading something about the government wanting to implant chips into every American so our whereabouts could always be tracked. I don't remember all the details but I do remember thinking about how well that wouldn't go and then I got to thinking about our usage of cell phones. In a sense, we're already "chipped." We've become so addicted and dependent on these little devices and over such a short period of time, haven't we? I'm not completely controlled by mine but I do use it. I wouldn't panic if I lost it or had to give it up as I choose not to store my entire existence on it. For me it's still just a handy way of knowing how Don's day is going without actually talking to him and a way to check my Facebook notifications and perhaps make a call.....to Russia!

Phones have really evolved. Land lines are becoming less standard all the time. I'm old fashioned in that sense and we do have a land line, but all of our phones are cordless. I can't say I miss being tied to a phone with a cord but when I was a kid, that was all we had. I don't remember party lines, but they were a normal part of conversing on the phone just before I had received my official training on how to make a call. Our downstairs phone sat on the big old wooden buffet in the corner of our dining room. It was a desk type model in a neutral tan color. It had a very short cord so you were pretty much situated in the corner of the dining room during all of your conversations. My mom sat our grade school pictures in their little fold out paper frames on that buffet along with the phone book and the old mantle clock dad had purchased at an auction sale. When any of us kids were on the phone we would fiddle around with that clock and doodle on the pages of the phone book. One time my brother decided to poke a pencil through my cheek on the kindergarten 5 x 7 glossy sitting in front of him while he exchanged words with a friend. I knew he hated me back then, but that was then and things are beginning to turn around now, so life is good. It only took 43 years. We never would have had this problem if I would have arrived before him. He really liked being the baby of the family. He had held that position for 4 years and had no idea he would be asked to give it up. My mom said that when they brought me home from the hospital, he sat on the steps and pouted and begged them to return me. When he realized they had lost the receipt and I was staying, things got very interesting.

I'll never forget the time when he talked my friend and me into standing inside the camper dad built, by the window, so he could throw water balloons at us. We were stupid enough to agree and we both stood there with our noses pushed up against the glass posing as his target. He was a bit of a rebel so he placed a "bullet" in each hand and what happened next taught all of us a very important lesson about quality merchandise. Back then, anything that wasn't made of glass was made to last, even balloons. They flew through the air with the greatest of ease but upon impact, they DIDN'T EXPLODE but rather fell to the ground intact, jiggling like something he'd become quite fond of in his approaching teen years! The glass camper window, however, shattered and sent my brother into "Dad is going to kill me!" mode. My friend and I were fine as there was a metal screen on the inside of the window protecting us from flying glass but it was definitely something that wasn't going to heal itself. Jr knew the glass would need to be replaced and he knew dad needed to know what happened so he played one of his "Mom, will you please tell dad?" cards and prayed dad would let him live. It always seemed like bad news coming from her was better than bad news coming from us. Not once did we see him spank her and although he claimed his entire life that he only needed to give each one of us one spanking, we definitely gave him reasons to rethink that decision many times during our childhood years. As an adult I can still remember him saying, "After each one of you got your spanking, you were expected to know better." He was right most of the time. We still messed up occasionally but not on purpose. I'm guessing our one spanking from him arrived because we were told "no" by mom and we didn't listen. I was so young when I got mine that I don't even remember it. I suppose that's good but it does sort of make me wonder about the rotten baby I must have been.

Looking back is so fun. Each and every one of us has a ton of memories from our childhood years and I'm so very thankful mine was what it was. Not once do I remember dad ever threatening to kill any of us but I do remember the tremendous amount of respect we had for him and that crossing his line just wasn't the thing to do.

Prevented Wrinkles

Having a big sister is wonderful. I've had mine now for almost 50 years and I wouldn't give her up for anything in the world. Oh, we've had our ups and downs over the years but most of the rough stuff was over and done with by the time I was 10. The only visible sign left from my younger years is a scar on my knee from a bicycle incident. Becky and I are both getting older and I'm starting to notice some facial wrinkles but come to think of it, I really don't have any incredibly deep furrows on my forehead and I think I may have just figured out why.

Every year we would get a nice assortment of gifts for Christmas. Our parents didn't spend hundreds of dollars on us but we always had presents under the tree and one year, my sister got a smoking hot steel rod complete with the optional "steam chamber." The box cleverly disguised this torture device by

74

calling it a "curling iron." I wish I had read the entire pamphlet that came with it as I'm almost 100% sure it had to have said something about using your little sister as a guinea pig before making any attempt to use it on yourself. Becky couldn't wait to get that curling iron out of the box and I was asked to be her first victim...err, ah, I mean customer. I found out that day trouble was headed my way each and every time my sister would say, "Oh come on. This will be fun."

It was almost as if she was preparing for surgery. First she unscrewed the tiny little tube from the end of the iron, filled it with water and then screwed it back into place. The cord on the opposite end was then inserted into the outlet. As the rod began to heat, it would slowly warm the water inside that little tube. When the hair was securely wrapped around the rod, the operator would then press the button on the steam tube. When pressed, it would send steam out of the holes in the wand that would help to "lock in" that gorgeous new curl. We both waited anxiously for the "hot" indicator to illuminate and when the "ready" light popped on it was time for me to take my seat on the toilet, close my eyes and wait patiently for the newest way to say hello to some quick and easy curls and goodbye to those nasty sponge rollers!

Slowly she parted off a section of my hair. She ran the comb through it a couple of times while I prayed for the safety of my hair, my head and my sanity. She wrapped her fingers around the handle of that smoking hot steel rod and the closer she got to my face, the more worried I got. I wanted to trust her but this was the woman that would never let me tag along with her and her friends and the woman that would never allow me to sit on her bed and the woman that caused a head on collision between me and my bike and her and her bike on my very first ride without training wheels. It was very obvious she wasn't doing this because she liked me but that kind of logic developed a bit later than my appointment. All I knew was she had a pretty good hold on my hair so there I sat. I flinched and squirmed as she made an attempt to attach my bangs to that rod. Eventually she got some hair in the clip and began to roll that torture device dangerously close to my forehead. I already knew I didn't like the heat radiating off that wand but we both knew I had to stick it out for at least 30 seconds if I wanted a curl. I had sort of forgotten about the steam feature due to the fact that I was concentrating so hard on the smoking hot steel rod that was perched dangerously close to my eyes but she hadn't and when she hit that tiny little button on the end of that rod, lightning bolts shot through my eye sockets and I'm still wondering why dad never had to patch the plaster above the toilet! There should have been a "head size" hole directly above that spot at the beauty shop!

I haven't seen a curling iron with the little steam tube option for years. I would be willing to bet they were discontinued after a short time on the market. I would also be willing to bet that if you were to ask every 49 year old woman that has almost no forehead furrows if she had a big sister that owned a curling iron with the optional "steam chamber," the answer would unanimously be "YES! How did you know?"

A Nice Slice Of Gravy

For many years Thanksgiving was celebrated at my parent's house, Christmas was celebrated at my sister's house and Easter became our holiday after I got married. I'll never forget the very first year I became the Easter hostess and I know the kitchen curtains and the drain in the sink won't either.

I'm not sure what I was thinking, but in those early years of entertaining I would wear myself out in an attempt to make everything as perfect as I possibly could. I remember cleaning every speck of dirt I could find and washing and pressing all the curtains and waxing the kitchen floor and washing all the throw rugs. By the time the holiday arrived I was almost too tired to stay awake and enjoy our guests.

When our first Easter had arrived I had been a homemaker for almost a year so I was hoping to impress my guests with my culinary skills. I remember my mother-in-law being the first to arrive. It was sort of nerve racking as she was a very good cook. Shortly after her arrival my parents came through the door and I knew the rest of our guests would not be far behind so I decided it would be a great time to begin my gravy. I sent both my mother and my mother-in-law into the dining room so I had plenty of room in our small kitchen to do what I needed to do. I remember both ladies offering advice on gravy making and I remember quite clearly that they both agreed using the potato water would be the thing to do. Well, that threw a wrench in my plans. Hmmm, should I listen or just go with the plan I had in place before they arrived. I decided I better give the potato water a try as I didn't want these more experienced cooks to think I thought I knew more than them so I filled my Tupperware shaker 3/4's full of the hot steamy potato water and added about 3/4's cup of corn starch. I put the little blending wheel at the top and then snapped the lid in place. I took hold of that innocent container and began to shake it. What happened next was one of the biggest shocks I have ever encountered. The shaker EXPLODED spewing hot potato water with corn starch chunks all over my clean, perfectly pressed kitchen curtains!! I would most likely never forget hot liquid in a Tupperware shaker was not a good idea so I opted to not jot down any notes for future gravy endeavors provided there were some.

Once my heart rate returned to a somewhat normal pace I opted to put Plan B in motion. It was the original plan I had for the gravy and there were no voices attempting to talk me out of it after witnessing what had just happened. I remember giving the shaker a second chance but this time I was using cold milk. We were both still a little tense when I started the shaking process but everything went fine and before I knew it, the milk and corn starch were perfectly blended and ready to pour into the turkey drippings waiting in the saucepan. Everything blended so nicely. As the gravy began to cook it took on an impressive smooth, velvety appearance with absolutely no lumps. This gravy was surely going to impress those two experienced cooks in the other room. I needed to smooth things over as I was worried they were still in a bit of shock due to all the screaming they heard when the first attempt blew up.

I remember pouring this glorious gravy into a bowl but before I sat it on the table I remember getting the salads and relish trays out of the refrigerator. About then, the rest of the family arrived so we got distracted for a few minutes and when I came back to the kitchen to grab the gravy I noticed something very strange. Liquids slosh around and this gravy was liquid but it wasn't sloshing. I found this very odd so I made an attempt to "dip" my finger into it and I discovered a problem. Apparently 3/4th's of a cup of corn starch is perhaps just a bit too much for gravy unless you're making enough for 75 people. During the time lapse from saucepan to bowl my gravy had turned into a solid mass much like the consistency of jellied cranberries! I surely wouldn't be able to serve it unless my guests were open to eating a slice of gravy so I made an attempt to dump it down the drain! Dump it, yeah right! I had to cut it in small pieces before the drain would even consider swallowing it!

Everyone survived our first Easter dinner including me. Everyone was fine without gravy that year. I switched to flour as my thickening agent and we've gotten along very well. I still have some corn starch in the cupboard but the chances of me using it again are quite slim. As for the boiling hot potato water, I effortlessly dump it down the drain every time I make gravy! I'm sure you can understand.

I Almost Expired!

There are times I think expiration dates on food items are completely ridiculous. Don and I most likely have several salad dressings, mustards and steak sauces in the refrigerator that have all expired and we continue to use them. We're still fine and neither of us has been sick with any vomiting issues so I say expiration dates on some things are pretty silly. It's just another way to control consumers I suppose. I do, however, respect the dates on refrigerator biscuits more than I used to. As you read on, you'll find out why.

I've never enjoyed the process of getting those pressurized refrigerator tubes open. Sometimes they'll pop when you peel the first layer of paper off the tube but other times they wait and continue to torment you by suggesting you poke the edge of a spoon up against that seam you see when you get the first layer of paper removed. You have to sort of wonder what kind of thought process goes into this kind of unpredictable packaging. The people that come up with ideas like this would have to have an incredibly warped sense of humor, don't you think?

I really can't remember why I decided to open that expired can of biscuits. Perhaps I was making beef stew and thought they would be a nice addition or maybe we were just out of bread and I didn't feel like running to the store. It's hard to say but it really doesn't matter. I took out the cookie sheet and misted it with a bit of cooking spray. I took hold of that tube and slowly began to peel the paper away and nothing happened. I reached for a spoon and braced myself for the POP! that was about to happen and nothing happened. Hmmm, I was stumped so I decided to whack that stubborn tube on the edge of the counter and what happened next is part of the reason I have gray hair and trust issues. The pressured contents literally EXPLODED AND BLEW THE BISCUITS TO BITS! There was biscuit shrapnel on my face, in my hair, on the counter, walls and ceiling but not a single bit on the awaiting greased cookie sheet! I'll never forget what happened when the seal let loose on that can. I'm going to mention that we didn't own a single gun at the time. We didn't have any fireworks left over from the 4th of July and we didn't have any propane leaks but the noise that had just come out of that "cannon" sounded like something much worse than what it was!

These biscuits aren't that expensive. If you find an expired can of them in your refrigerator, please take my advice and place them gently into the garbage. Gently people.... gently.

Not Before Work

As a result of a car accident several years ago, Don has had issues with his back. While away for work, he and I got in a conversation about mattresses and due to the fact that his back had been a bit worse lately he asked if I would go and scope out a few just to see what's available. I thought it was a good idea as the one we are currently sleeping on is getting old and a little worn. I had the morning off the following day so I decided I would check out the mattress store that was close to where I work first just to see what they had available. I learned that shopping for a new mattress before going to work is probably not the best idea I've ever had. In the "narrow down the possibilities" process I was asked to lay on at least 10 beds. Do you have any idea what that does to a hairdo? Initially I thought the salesperson was a bit over the top with her glittery eye shadow, glittery nails, sequin sweater, studded leggings and glittery boots but I gave new meaning to the word tacky after that shopping experience! I looked like I had just removed my head from the inside of a vacuum and my clothes took on that "I forgot to get you folded when the dryer stopped" appearance! This really helped me to realize why we wear pajamas to bed. Our street clothes have no idea how to act when asked to pose as pajamas. They fail miserably. My jeans were situated in a place they had no business being and my shoulder pads had slipped off my shoulders and I'm not so sure I didn't lose an earring. The $3500 estimate "Sparkle" scratched on the back of her business card activated the thrifty side of my brain immediately and I unearthed a much less expensive option that could turn our existing bed into one that felt just as good as the one from the "hair messing and clothes shuffling" store I had stopped at before work. Don pondered my idea for a few days and eventually his back talked him into my less expensive plan.

When I returned from the store, I was lugging a box into the house weighing more than it looked like it should have. It was getting close to bedtime so Don plopped our new purchase on the bed and opened the box. What we found inside was something that resembled one of the biggest blobs of chewed bubble gum we had ever seen. It was supposed to eventually become a three inch thick memory foam topper but it was definitely going to need some time to breath before it would be able to convince us it was going to look anything like the picture on the box.

Several weeks have passed and I can honestly say, memory foam takes some getting used to. It has an almost "quicksand" effect. It's as hard as a rock when you touch it but it really does seem to eliminate stress points. I learned all about stress points when I was at the bed store. The first few nights we felt as if we were sleeping in our very own little cocoons! I believe we are both beyond the "getting used to it" phase and neither of us has decided that sinking into our cocoons each night is a bad thing. It didn't take me long to realize I needed to be facing the edge of the bed before deciding to get up as rolling over and getting off the bed aren't as easy as when you are removing yourself from a regular mattress. After this experience I have an all new appreciation for caterpillars that enter into their cocoon phase. They would really have to be prepared if they planned to take a lot of potty breaks while earning their wings!

Today I am going to add a dust ruffle to our bed. Don and I have been talking about this for quite some time so I think he is ready to handle this part of the bedroom "bevitization" that is going to take place today. I have always loved to re-purpose things and a few weeks ago I found 445" inches of cream colored batten-burg lace valances at a secondhand store. This will be enough to make a dust ruffle and trim for pillow shams. When I divulged my plan to the gals at the store they said, "We want pictures!" I love how other women can relate to things like this. I knew Don would be okay with it too so the fact that he is 1383.5

miles away for at least another 32 hours was no part of the planning process! (Okay, that's not true!)

Bed Plop Belly Flop

If you ever plan to take an 11 year old girl shopping, you will be in for an experience that will definitely entertain you and if the 11 year old you take is anything like the one Don and I took, you will not be bored.

Gabby is one of the most beautiful young souls that has ever touched my heart and I cherish every second I've been able to spend with her. She and I met when I moved back to my hometown to begin the cleansing period I felt I needed after going through a divorce. Not long after meeting her, I met Don and the three of us have all become very good friends. Don and I are so happy Gabby's dad is willing to share her with us as she is a such a peach! It wasn't uncommon for us to take her shopping with us when Don would come to visit for the weekend. One of those times we shopped for a Halloween costume and it didn't take me long to realize how an 11 year old and a 48 year old's opinions would differ! There may have been a bit of teeth gritting at the secondhand store when every dress I showed her received the same response, "Nope, it looks like a grandma dress." Don saved the day and my sanity when he found the perfect Zombie Bride costume for her at one of the discount stores we stopped at and it only needed a minimal amount of tweaking before it passed her inspection.

On a different weekend Don felt the bed I was sleeping on needed to be replaced so we picked up Gabby and headed to the nearest bed selling town. Don is not the type that likes to shop around for long periods of time so we got right down to business and found the mattress section in the store. I laid on a few different possibilities and eventually found a rather reasonably priced one that felt like it would probably do the trick. Before long Don was standing at the checkout counter. I was somewhere between him and Gabby. She was shopping around and spotted an enormous king size bed in one of the bedroom furniture sections. It was all decked out with a nice fluffy comforter and all I remember, as I tossed a glance in her direction, was the plummet. She decided this bed was calling her name so she positioned herself at the foot of it, held out her arms as if she was flying and let herself drop. It didn't take us long to realize there was no mattress under that comforter but rather a nice slab of plywood! What a shock! Wouldn't you think a store that sells mattresses would have one set up in every bedroom furniture grouping? Apparently not. I was glad Gabby didn't get hurt and after the fact we laughed and laughed. I don't think Don saw it happen but I'm sure he heard the thud when the faux mattress found its victim!

On the way home Gabby was attempting to send a text to a friend and her phone kept typing multiplies of the same letter and she said, "Ugh! I hate it when my phone stutters!" I actually thought that was a rather creative way to explain the issue she was having and that too, made us laugh.

I have no children of my own but what I've learned from Gabby and the numerous hours we've spent together is that they like their phones, their games and their brand name clothes but I'm willing to bet most of them would trade it all if it meant they would get more time to spend with someone that truly cares about them. I'm thinking this would be especially true if that someone is willing to listen when they need to talk, someone that wants to blow bubbles, make scarves, help with homework, make a jump rope out of old Walmart bags and take them mattress shopping. I was that person for Gabby and I will cherish those times for the rest of my life and honestly, I think she will too!

It Runs

Every day, as I head off to work, I drive past a parking lot filled with shiny new and slightly used vehicles. At first glance one might think it's an automobile dealership but it's a parking lot for the adjacent high school. I'm not jealous that all of those teens are driving vehicles nicer than most of the ones I owned before I was 30 but you sort of have to wonder how many have actually been given the responsibility of making the payments. My parents weren't able to provide any of us with wheels. There was always a bus to ride and once in a while we rode with a friend that was borrowing their parent's car or actually scraping up payments for one of their own.

I didn't get bitten by the "car" bug until I received a job offer that was 35 miles from where I lived. I knew walking was out of the question and carpooling might work but I'm sure the willing party would expect me to drive sometimes and I knew I would eventually run out of excuses when it was actually my turn to drive. Anyone with even the tiniest amount of common sense would get a bit suspicious if I had a flat tire every other Monday when it was my turn to pick them up.

My dad didn't spend a second worrying about my wheels or lack thereof but my brother did. I'm not sure why as he had never spent a lot of his time bonding with me unless you can call throwing me off the back of his snowmobile every time he offered to give me a ride to my friend's house bonding. He's in his mid 50's now and I still don't fully understand how his brain works. I appreciate what he's done for me and perhaps someday I will actually be able to "figure" him out. He just told me he was tired of me driving mom's car so he took it upon himself to lead me in the direction of some very affordable wheels.

I'll never forget the night I first laid eyes on something that would land me my very first "honest face" loan at the bank. It was late in the afternoon when Jr stopped by and asked if I wanted to buy a car. He had located a 1974 Plymouth Volare up in North Dakota. He had no idea if this would be the perfect car for me but he was willing to take me to the little old farmer's place to check it out. We knew it was in running condition and due to the fact this requirement was at the very top of my list, we headed north.

It was half past dark when we drove in the yard at the old farmer's place and the only light available was a distant dusk to dawn light and a few rays streaming from the kitchen window. What I saw resembled a car and it appeared to be red with a beige top. It was a two door and the engine came to life once the key was turned. Both headlights and taillights worked. It was quite clean and after a very short mechanical inspection Jr said, "Well, it's up to you but the guy wants $350 for it and I'll co-sign a loan at the bank if you want it." It wasn't long and we were rolling down the driveway with a car I had just written a rubber check for, praying the bank would loan me the money the following day. Jr only let me do this as he had the money to cover my check if the bank wouldn't. I can't say I wasn't excited. I'm quite sure the kids that get the new cars handed to them are excited too but this kind of excitement was the kind that put the fear of God in you because you knew you had finally reached the point in life that had awarded you with a brand new set of responsibilities!

I'm not sure I slept at all that first night. My car....m-y v-e-r-y o-w-n c-a-r was sitting out beside the house!!! I worried about my meeting at the bank and then I worried about insurance and then I worried about having gas money. I worried about everything I could possibly think of except the water pump. When my dad came in the house after doing a few things outside the next morning and told me my car was sitting in a pool of water due to the fact that the water pump went out devastation hit! Life, as I knew it, was over. My bubble had been burst. My financial obligations had just gone from scary to I NEED TO WIN THE LOTTERY!

Needless to say, the new water pump wasn't that expensive and Jr was willing to replace it, saving me labor costs. I did get approved for a loan at the bank and I'm quite sure the banker chuckled a little when he saw how terrified I was "signing my life away!" I sort of think he just took the money out of his personal account as he called it "An Honest Face" loan. I didn't miss a single $65 monthly payment at the bank so I had set the groundwork for being a good risk for future loans and when it came time to trade up my brother told me, "That car didn't cost you a dime." I didn't know then but I know now, just exactly what he was talking about. I drove that car back and forth to work, 70 miles a day round trip, for several years and the only thing I put into it was a water pump and a thermostat. After seeing it in the daylight, I joked about the fact that it was 10% car and 90% body putty. It was obviously in an accident that caused the rear end an extensive amount of damage but it still ran. I did drive it one whole winter without heat but that probably did more good than harm as it helped me to be thankful for every car that had a working heater after that.

Now I'm driving a very nice car. Everything works and it is definitely costing me a whole lot more than $350 but I wouldn't trade my experience I had with my old Volare for anything in the world. It taught me to be thankful for having a mechanic for a brother. It taught me to be humble, as it delivered a hefty dose of humility every time I got out of it when there were people around. It taught me to never take anything for granted and it taught me that not having everything handed to me most likely helped me to build a very solid foundation within myself that I have relied on for many years since.

The "Drop Off" Plan

My sister and I have come up with lots of great weight loss ideas together. We've tried lots of different things but the best idea to date was back in 2005 when we decided to give Weight Watchers a whirl. The program was easy to follow and we both enjoyed admirable results. We've both slipped a bit since then like almost every person that ever loses weight but I've been able to keep 110 pounds off for nearly ten years now. Although this makes me very happy I still have an ongoing desire to unleash the pounds that searched endlessly until they were able to find me once again. My knees and hips have had a very hard time understanding why losing a parent and going through a divorce and moving a couple of times in the past several years should have had anything to do with making myself so incredibly visible to those nasty pounds I hoped I had lost forever. I realize I will probably need to re-join the "accountability" team eventually but the exact date of that decision has not yet been determined. I will never forget some of the ideas for shedding unwanted pounds that have surfaced over the years and the first one, I remember, was created by the "sister and me" team.

We were both living in the same town at the time and we decided we would meet at the bank corner and go for a walk together, every morning. It was a sure fire way to get our bodies in fat burning mode for the entire day. It was going to be the perfect plan and we knew it. We could almost feel those unwanted pounds falling off our bodies on Day One as we snapped off our alarm clocks and hopped out of bed. I laid my walking clothes out the night before so it wasn't long and I was heading down the road to meet my sister. Day One went great! This was such a wonderful plan. The only thing that bothered us is why we hadn't thought of it sooner........then, Day Two arrived.

One would think Day Two would arrive with at least 50% of the adrenalin that Day One had produced but that didn't seem to be the case. Becky and I were both a lot fonder of the evening hours part of a day than we were with the morning hours part of a day but she had a couple of small children so she had somewhat adapted. I, on the other hand, had not. I will most likely never forget how Day Two began. Apparently I had stayed up a little later than I should have at the end of Day One and I distinctly remember what woke me up and it wasn't my alarm clock. Unfortunately it was my sister standing at the foot of my creaky old brass bed asking me if I had any immediate plans of GETTING OUT OF IT!!!! It's safe to say, the getting up and meeting Becky part wasn't going to be 100% reliable so I took about 13 years off before coming up with another weight loss and fitness plan.

Every day my husband would drive 9 miles to work. I decided that if I got up and rode with him and had him drop me off a few miles from town that my only choice would be to walk if I wanted to get back home. This plan was most likely going to be the one I would end up discussing with Oprah when my success story hit the airwaves. I envisioned Oprah paging through the brightly illustrated "Get Dropped Off and Drop The Weight" manual I would create and witness the moment when she said everyone in her audience would be going home with their very own copy of my brightly illustrated weight loss and fitness guide! I have these "Walter Mitty" type moments quite often and this was surely one of them.

The plan really did seem quite amazing. What I didn't know is there would be a glitch. There was a farmer that lived on the outskirts of town that we passed every day before my "drop off" point and he had cattle. The place he lived on was a sight for sore eyes and rumor had it he did a fair share of his mechanic type tinkering while seated at the kitchen table. He wasn't a bad guy but there were quality issues with nearly everything he touched. One of those issues included his ability to build a fence that actually kept cattle in. I'm not sure how much time you've ever spent around cattle but they're curious creatures and when they notice something a bit different during their day, they will investigate. Unfortunately I was that "something different" when I started walking past their field of vision and they investigated. What I didn't realize is that several of those cows had new calves and due to the fact that the fence was not meeting "keep the calves in" standards I had a calf following me down the road. There were cars meeting me and an uncomfortable number of the drivers were pointing and laughing as they strolled by. Initially this made me feel a bit more self-conscious than usual but eventually the BALLER I heard from behind helped me to realize I had picked up a little friend that had a mother that was not one bit impressed with the fact that her baby fit through the hole in the fence but she didn't!

It's safe to say my plan for weight loss and fitness had flopped again. I don't have a lot of fears but unfortunately being chased by a cow is one of them and I wasn't willing to risk being joined by momma cow when the fence completely failed had I continued with my "Drop Off" plan.

Unfortunately I'm still carrying some extra weight that will eventually come off. I've learned that taking small steps each and every day help tremendously in the long run. I may be willing to revisit the "Drop Off" plan someday, after all, what are the chances of being chased by a cow again while out for a walk? I must say this experience fostered significant growth in my spiritually. In my mind I was being followed by a 2500 pound bull but in reality it was a very spunky, fun loving calf that wanted to play. It sort of puts a lot of things about life in perspective. We almost always tend think the worst first and often times use prayer as a last resort. Experiences like this have a way of shifting your thought process into one that knows the worst has definitely not happened yet but the possibility exists and saying a prayer is the first thing that will pop into your mind! Everything turned out fine and I can honestly say it helped me to be just a bit more trusting when it comes to who's in charge!

His Aim Was Spot On

I had a nosebleed the other day and for some reason it made me think of two separate memories. How strange is that? I know, it's strange but the memories are sort of funny....sort of.....okay, maybe for an innocent bystander. The first one was when my big sister became a contestant in a spelling bee. I'm not sure what grade she was in but I'm guessing it was maybe third. The word she was asked to spell was blood. She thought for a moment and then proceeded. BLOOD, B-L-U-D, BLOOD. I have no memory of being there and if she was 8, I was only 3 so I wouldn't have caught her goof anyway but every time she tells this story I laugh. It was probably tragic for her as there were no awards given at a competition like that back then if you spelled something wrong. It wasn't like some places today when awards are given to every child so nobody feels bad. I can't say I wouldn't have liked it that way back when I was a kid but being told no and not winning at everything did have its rewards. I guess it formed our backbones and I can honestly say mine has definitely come in handy!

The second memory is a bit graphic and requires a bit of setup so here goes. The old house we grew up in only had two bedrooms so my dad built a dividing wall down the middle of the bigger one. Half of it became my sister's and my room and the other half became my brother's room. The bedroom only had one door on it so in order to create a bit of privacy for my brother, my mom strung a curtain across his section. There was only one closet too and that was on his side so getting clothes out of it was never easy. He was very picky about who came in his room and when you knocked on the curtain and asked, the answer was almost always NO! I can't remember for sure but I'm betting mom didn't have a lot of laundry for Becky and me back then as we most likely wore the same outfit for several days due to the fact that the majority of our clothes were being held hostage in the unattainable closet! My sister and I avoided Jr's room and him as much as possible because we were never quite sure what he was up to. At a very young age he was showing a deep appreciation for sling shots and pop guns and we just never knew what might follow and just who he might choose as his first target.

When I had that nosebleed I remembered a day, years ago, when my brother decided to work on his marksmanship skills. It was a bit unfortunate that he was the only one that knew anything about this plan on that particular day but he had recently acquired a brand new suction cup dart shooting gun and we sort of knew it wouldn't be long before he began his search for the perfect target. He has always loved guns but as a child that was most likely no older than 5 or 6, he wasn't aware that pointing guns at people was wrong even if they were your sisters. On the day of the incident, he opened his curtain door and noticed neither Becky nor I were in our room which immediately sparked the idea for a hunt. He loaded a dart in his new gun and began sneaking out of his room. Four feet later he found himself slinking up next to the bedroom door that led into the bathroom. He poked his head around the corner ever so discreetly and caught site of the perfect target perched on the toilet. In a matter of seconds he aimed, pulled the trigger and WHAMMO! He hit the bull's eye! This bull's eye's name was Becky and she was not the least bit impressed nor would anyone be if they got hit smack dab in the nose with a suction cup dart! Thankfully she survived but we weren't sure, at that point, if our devious brother would once this breaking news made its way to dad's ears! It was an unfortunate event but she really couldn't have been in a better place to suffer such a shock like that. There was toilet paper right next to her and the perfect seat should anything slip out....err, ah, well, you know what I mean. I don't think my sister will ever forget that day and I would also be willing to bet that she never misspelled Blood ever again. Not every unexpected event produces better spelling skills but this one certainly did! Blood, B-L-O-O-D, Blood.

Listening With One Ear

Isn't it funny how an object or scent or even a sound can bring back a memory? Tonight I was sitting on the couch after work and I caught sight of the tuft of pheasant feathers Don hung above the hutch and it took me back to the Sunday hunting trip he and I took late last fall.

As we were gathering the things we would need, he suggested I bring the camera as he was sure we would see some shots worth snapping as we searched for pheasants and then he said something about having the pickup window down a lot which triggered an overwhelming desire in me to dress warm. As I was deciding on the number layers to wear I remember him saying some other things too but apparently, I was not listening with both ears. I found out later that only half listening to those other things he was saying could have put my future hunting adventures with him in jeopardy but when all was said and done, he still loved me.

With that being said we headed west and south and east and north and then south again and before long, I was lost. It was a very chilly and windy fall day so the pheasants weren't out and about like they are on the nicer days. Our eyes searched many miles of fields and road ditches and finally we spotted a bird! Don drove ahead and then turned around, grabbed his gun, hopped out of the pickup, ran down the ditch and POW!!! The pheasant dropped from the sky and immediately Don headed into the field to retrieve it. I was totally amazed by what I had just witnessed. If I had tried this I would have fallen out of the pickup, stumbled into the ditch, forgot the gun and scared the pheasant into the next county. Due to the fact that it was Don that did the shooting I received the opportunity to watch him grab the bird but rather than head back to the pickup he started walking away and before long he was out of sight. It wasn't long after he disappeared that I saw several pheasants flying over but knew I had no way of telling him he was heading the wrong way so I grabbed the camera and snapped a few pictures. I could hardly wait to tell him about my pictures! I knew he was going to be thrilled. A while later I heard a gunshot which told me he found some pheasants but I was a bit distracted with the camera. Eventually I glanced in front of the pickup and saw him walking my way. I'm not sure why but some of the words he had mentioned earlier were sort of sinking in. I snapped a few pictures of him as he looked so cute in his hunting clothes but then I thought, he might have said something about me driving the pickup ahead if he should end up walking as it was very cold. I quickly hopped out of the passenger seat and as I began my walk around the front end of the pickup I heard him say, "It's a little late!!!!" Oops, I had waited too long. He was really close. When he got back to the pickup I remember seeing someone that would remind you of the cartoon character you would get if you threw Yosemite Sam and The Tasmanian Devil into a blender. His ears were nearly frozen and the gun shot I heard was to get my attention and apparently I had single handedly blown his "plan" all to hell! One thing I love about this man is that when he's mad, he's mad RIGHT NOW and when it's over, it's over. The rest of the trip went really smooth. His butt didn't leave the pickup seat until we got home and when I zoomed in on the pictures I took of him walking in that ditch half frozen, torqued to oblivion but looking really cute and the one I took of him holding his dead pheasant when we got home, they almost look like the same guy!

I suppose it's good the next pheasant hunting season is a spring and a summer and half of a fall away yet which will give Don's frozen ears plenty of time to "warm up" to the idea of giving me another chance to go hunting.

10,000 A Day

I have a personality sort of like the weather. It seems it's always changing and hopefully not terribly predictable except to one guy! I have my sunny moments and my rainy days. I have calm moments and if you ask Don he would most likely tell you I can be a bit breezy at times!

When I first moved in with Don, I crossed a state line, quit my job and moved to a city where I knew no one. The first few months were a bit rough and I still laugh when I recall the reason Don came up with for my feelings of sadness and isolation. I was used to working. I hadn't been unemployed since third grade. I so wanted to enjoy the two months off I was giving myself but fear of finding a job consumed me. I was used to getting up in the morning and I was used to chattering all day long with people and Don determined that I have a need to exchange at least 10,000 words a day in order to be happy. On the days when the minimum has not been met, he knows. He's an incredibly focused man so he gives his all to whatever it is he is doing. When he's watching television, he watches television. If I make an attempt to chat with him he will mute the tv and give me his undivided attention. Once I finish my thought he will usually ask me if I'm done and then continue on with what he was watching. When he's brushing his teeth, he's brushing his teeth. I'm not sure why but that is one of my favorite times to unload a bunch of information and I always forget that he's going to say, "I can't make out what you're saying. I'm brushing my teeth. When he's ready for bed, he's ready for bed. If I continue talking when he's trying to sleep he will usually say, "You didn't make it to 10,000 today, did you?" It's unfortunate, but on this one, he's probably right. I've never had anyone in my life that was able to decipher my intricately woven code until now. I suppose I could let this bother me but it really doesn't. The bottom line is he thinks I talk a lot. We have tons of wonderful conversations but on the days my minimum has not been met, I make several attempts to meet my quota and he is the lucky recipient of all those residual thoughts I feel I must shower upon at least two listening ears! He doesn't always willingly offer them but he is someone that comforts me when I'm "rainy", shares my "sunshine"and he's predicting a wonderful future for us in the years ahead!

Just A Bottle of Pink Paint

Every day when I head off to work I know I'm going to face at least one person that will make an attempt to gain access to the hidden counselor inside me. Each and every one of them finds their own unique way of hooking my attention and reeling me in. Yesterday that customer was a tall blonde woman in her late 50's. She appeared and began asking innocent questions about paint. I've done a lot of painting in my life so I was more than happy to offer my advice.

Before long I knew she had two sons that were both in college and that she had a friend that liked pigs. I found out the fascinating silver pots that sit on the table near the back corner of her deck were actually faded plastic and she spray painted them with the most beautiful silver spray paint ever made! She was the envy of all her friends and I knew this by the sparkle in her eye when she was telling me about each one of their individual compliments. Before long the conversation shifted to the faded mesh pub height deck chairs she purchased at a garage sale a few years ago and I was asked what she might do to brighten them up. Apparently the chairs get very little use but it's nice having them for the times when they entertain. Extra seating is always nice.

I'm not sure how a conversation can go from advice on paint, to kids in college, to spray painted pots, to talking about faded mesh on deck chairs, to microwavable potholders with mitered corners but that's the direction we headed next. Before long I heard about the friend that used the wrong kind of batting and ended up having a lightning storm inside of her microwave! The friend was mortified due to the fact that she had made lots of them before Christmas and gave almost all of them away as gifts! I also learned that if you have a microwave that doubles as a convection oven you don't have to worry about your gift from your "pot holder making" friend as it's only the microwaves that are just microwaves that seem to have the issues with lightening bouncing off the mitered corner pot holders housing the "stormy" batting. I also received a brief summary on the lightening occurrences and it was determined that the first use was the worst and the storm calmed considerably during the second and future uses of these handy creations! I am almost 100% sure I slept better last night just knowing this.

I learned that my patient....err, ah, I mean customer was not at all artistic but she did create some painted dish towels for her sons to use at college. She was shocked when she learned they were never dampened with the residual water from washed dishes but

98

rather perceived as artwork and her boys insisted she help them determine the best method for hanging those masterpieces! Her pig loving friend caught wind of this dish towel art and immediately offered herself as the next recipient of one of these frame worthy creations so the pink paint that was originally seated in the palm of the hand of my customer that had a few questions about it was well on its way to becoming an element of utmost importance needed to create the magnificent, the awe inspiring, the grand "Pig-casso!"

Life should never be boring. If you find it boring you are doing something wrong. If you're struggling miserably and have no idea how to eliminate this boredom, work retail! I'm not going to say you'll always love it but I am going to say, you will never be bored!

Crafty Counseling Service

Today's episode of "The Crafty Counselor" differs greatly from yesterday. Today I had a visit with a customer about fleece off the bolt versus fleece remnant prices and before I knew it she was telling me everyone in her family suffers from arthritis. I told her I had it too and about then I slipped in a comment about my toe as it gave me a little jab. Apparently about 3 or 4 months ago I dropped something on my big toe that caused the nail to turn black and today 3/4's of the old nail was ready to be removed. The new nail isn't fully formed yet so my toe decided to complain just a bit once it realized it had been stuffed in a sock and then a shoe without it's protective cover. All of a sudden the counselor role I typically play shifted and the lady I was visiting with came to my aide. She reached in her pocket and whipped out a tube of dollar store brand toothache gel and said, "Here, take your shoe off and slap some of this on that toe. Your pain will be a thing of the past." I tactfully refused but thanked her for her suggestion. She said "Well you'll have to remember this idea for another time. It's not just for teeth and gums ya know, it takes away any pain, any time." I'm glad our thoughts aren't visible as I had a brief moment when I envisioned rubbing this remedy on some of the people that tend to make my life miserable. They can be a real pain....a different kind but it still might be worth a try!

After the dollar store brand Orajel offering, the woman remembered I said I had arthritis and continued with her quest to give me comfort from my every affliction. She told me about something she was wearing but in order for me to see it, she would have to drop her pants. Can you honestly believe things like this happen at a fabric store? I was relieved when she confirmed that the pants were staying where they were but proceeded to have a rather heated argument with her phone until it brought up an image of the battery pack and four wires that her company makes to help alleviate pain. It looked rather interesting but I had to cut our session short as there were other people backed up awaiting their session with "The Crafty Counselor." They had no idea what they were in for should they mention any issues they have been experiencing with pain. I was ready. I had answers!

Waiting On A Woman

I'm not sure why, but for some reason I have never been terribly fond of doing things until I absolutely need to. Some would call this procrastination. I call it a method in which to live by. This characteristic of my personality drives Don bananas. A while back we were planning to head south for the weekend. Don typically works until 4:00 and I was going to be off at 12:30 that day which would give me ample time to pick up a few things at the grocery store, alter my jeans, let the hem down on one of my tops and hem the sleeves on my jacket, tidy up the house and get our bags packed. Don threw me a curve ball mid-morning when he sent a text informing me he was getting off early and that I should "be prepared." I asked him what early meant and his response turned up a 2:30ish comment. I quickly adjusted my plan of attack and decided 2:30ish was surely going to fall somewhere between 2:31-2:59. I chose 2:48 and moved on with my calculations. I added the time it would take for him to drive home from work and the time it would take for him to shower and assemble the things he wanted to take which brought me to an approximate departure time that was very near what I had originally planned so I sent him a text that said his "get off" time should work out perfectly. He had no clue about all the figuring I had done nor did he have any idea he would hear the hum of my sewing machine when he walked in the door.

I realized there would be a certain degree of schmoozing necessary as with any plan between a man and a woman when the woman is me and the man is him so I decided to add something to my list that wasn't originally there. This was my buffer to protect me should he arrive sooner than expected. I've learned it's important to let this addition be something you're doing for him. That always seems to work well. On this particular occasion we were planning to attend a fund raising event the following evening hence the alterations on my clothes and I noticed his new jeans were in need of hemming so I added them to my sewing pile. Another time buyer is hoping they will think of something you can do for them. Due to the fact that it was our brother-in-law's birthday, I distracted him by asking him to write on the card which prompted him to get creative and he asked me to whip up a small bag for the gold coins he wanted to give as a birthday gift. This was working out so well for me but he still felt the need to deliver several "Let's go! "comments which ended up making him look like a very predictable and mixed up cuckoo clock! He popped in the office/sewing room every 3 minutes as a matter of fact! A very common response I tend to use is "Where's the fire?" and another one I like is "Everything is going to work out just fine." I use these quite often and I'm getting sort of fond of the deep, low pitched growl that comes out of him following my comments!

Eventually we left town and reached our destination with plenty of time to do what needed doing. Don mentioned that song about "Waitin on a woman" once we were on the road and he was all in favor of me writing about our time clashes. He loves to complain about my procrastination and he loves to believe that one day he will change me but I also believe he understands the lyrics of that song and that he knows waiting for me will never be a waste of his time.

An Appliance With An Attitude

There is really no way to ever know just exactly what your day will bring. Sometimes I begin my day by dropping everything I attempt to pick up. Sometimes I oversleep. Sometimes I hit the snooze button several times and sometimes I actually get up before the alarm goes off. Yes, that has actually happened. Maybe like 3 times if you must know, but they count!

And then there was a morning not long ago when I thought I was ready to surprise Don with a hot steamy cup of fresh coffee. He usually makes his own but I thought he might like not having to wait for it to brew. I planned this little surprise the night before so that all I would have to do is crawl out of bed, walk down the hall and push the button on Mr. Coffee. When Don finished showering I knew his nose would lead him into the kitchen with a silly smile on his sleepy face murmuring the word "cooooffffeeeeee." The sweet surprise took a rather unexpected turn and that was the day I learned Mr. Coffee had an attitude. I found out that he prefers the carafe to be in a certain position and if it's not, he will pump all of the water in his water holding area onto the counter rather than allowing it to flow over the coffee grounds and into the carafe. Now I'm not the type to scream and yell and throw things. I'm the type that gets upset, utters a few choice words about product quality to the hypothetical manufacturer that is located somewhere near the ceiling and then I walk away. On this particular occasion I'm quite sure Mr. Coffee thought he had won. I'm quite sure he was already thinking about trying this again. He had no idea that my "Kodak" moment was developing and that it would force him to be sorry. You might be thinking revenge but I prefer to call it "a plan to defuse" in this case, a rather devious appliance.

I knew my plan would be most successful if implemented when I was home alone. Lucky for me, Don's work schedule was going to require him to be gone for a few days when Mr. Coffee and his attitude were still very fresh on my mind. I waited for Don to roll his suitcase across the deck and when I heard the pickup door shut and the engine start I knew it was time to put my plan in motion!

I peeked around the corner from the living room and I could see Mr. Fussypants sitting there on the counter. He was all cocky with his aqua lighted time glowing on the sleek black display panel. His water chamber was empty so he wasn't able to pull any of his hi-jinks on me but I know he wanted to. He knew the guy he made coffee for had left and perhaps he didn't like me because I don't like coffee. Maybe it was personal. For a brief second I felt a bit of compassion for him. Maybe I made him feel bad and maybe I should put an end to my plan and apologize to him. Thankfully those thoughts were extinguished by the memory of the pile of wet towels we used to clean up his mess on the morning he decided to have an attitude!

I hope this won't change how you perceive me but I walked up to the counter. I took hold of the plug on the end of Mr. Coffee's cord and I gave it a rather rapid tug and before he knew what had happened, he was rendered lifeless! His aqua lighted time glowing on his sleek black display panel faded away. That little dab of electricity he was so used to sipping on throughout the day was gone! I huffed a bit of breath onto my fingernails and buffed it away and said to him, "I guess it's safe to say you won't be having any more "light bulb" moments on how to mess with me now that I have removed your power!" This comment was followed by a rather devious bout of laughter as I walked out of the room.....bahahahahahaha! When I was a safe distance from Mr. No-Coffee I said, "I win! "and then I laughed again!

When Don returned home he noticed the coffee pot was unplugged and asked, "What's up with this?" I told him I had trust issues with that devious machine and then I winked at Mr. No-Coffee and headed down the hall to get ready for bed.

Angels Among Us

Today didn't get off to a bad start. I only hit the snooze button once. I was showered and ready for work early and the sun was shining. My workday started out quite slow but eventually the flow of customers began to pick up and before long I found myself having some rather interesting chats as I typically do. I really didn't expect anything all that special to happen but that's when it usually does.

Two ladies approached the checkout. One was probably in her late 70's and the other was most likely in her 50's. I remember the older of the two asking me about the availability of a product they weren't able to locate in the store and I suggested they check our website. The older lady said, "That's what everyone says. Check the website, check the website. I get so tired of hearing that suggestion." I agreed with her and then our conversation shifted into one about a business down the street closing and how hard it is to keep businesses staffed and also how difficult it is to find reliable workers. I commented about how surprised I was at how low the pay for jobs can be in a city this size and then I uttered something about wondering why I was even working where I was, knowing that I would never be able to get ahead with what I make. The elderly lady nodded in agreement and started to walk away. The younger one looked at me and with one of the most sincere and heartfelt tones I have ever heard she said, "God has an amazing plan for you." She walked a few steps and then looked back at me with a reassuring smile that filled me with peace. It was almost as if she was checking me off the list she was assigned this morning before she left Heaven.

I do honestly believe there are angels among us. The one I visited with today had beautiful brown hair, sparkling brown eyes, a pleasant smile and a few simple, yet powerful words of encouragement for a woman that sometimes allows herself to believe she will never get ahead and that she has nothing all that special to offer the world.

I loved today. I hope you did too.

April's Fool

I'm not sure about you, but I did my taxes on April Fool's Day. It's sort helps to alleviate the pain involved when the government takes money from you if you tell yourself "April Fool's!" They still take your money but it feels better when you think they're joking.

Everything went quite well but my brain was a bit overwhelmed. I say this because of the dreams I had when I finally dozed off. I used a popular online source for my tax preparations and their processes are incredibly thorough. I can honestly say I'm glad they ask you several hundred questions but up until that night I had never been asked if I had money deposited in a foreign bank account. All I could think was I wish they had an "I wish" button, but they didn't. I was up until 3 am and when I went to bed, this is what happened in my head once I drifted off to sleep.

Due to the fact that these dreams were so ridiculous, I am going to add some "logic" to parts of them that might help to explain where some of the colorful details came from. These will be bits and pieces from my previous day and general statements that may sort of tie things together. They will be situated between the brackets. I am also going to add some thoughts that would

106

have transpired if the dreams would have actually been true. They will be featured in the areas between the parentheses.

[I'm going to work on my taxes much earlier in the day next year so the chances of having dreams like these are less likely to happen again.]

That was a sample of a thought much like the others you will see in brackets. Those thoughts will be true statements. I just want to get you prepared.

Dream: It all started out when one of the women I work with found out that she was going to be a grandma.

[We have a ton of customers that purchase fabric for receiving blankets and burp clothes which might explain why there was going to be a baby.]

Dream: When the baby arrived she found out her son's girlfriend abandoned it at the hospital. She brought the baby to work and gave it to me. I remember being very concerned about what to feed the baby and I remember it being wrapped in a blanket made from royal blue tie dyed blizzard fleece.

[We sell a ton of blizzard fleece and I sold some of the royal blue to someone recently so that explains the baby's blanket.]

(Don has been gone all week for work. I typically use these times to make a few changes in the house but adding a baby has never crossed my mind. He claims to be very observant but he does miss a few things from time to time. I think it's safe to say he wouldn't miss this little surprise.)

Dream: All of a sudden I was shopping at Walmart. I suppose I was stocking up on diapers and formula and I noticed the work attire had drastically changed. The employees were wearing maroon and gold satin robes and large sequined hats. I can't even begin to explain my reaction. As I began to slowly recover from my visual shock I was approached by an elderly lady. She mistook me for an employee and began grilling me on why the regular price of a three pack of men's t shirts were less expensive than the ones on clearance and ended up storming off to the checkouts with the more expensive clearance ones.

[We have cranky confused customers all the time in our store and sometimes the decisions they make, make no sense.]

Dream: In a flash I walking down the street past the old school I attended through the sixth grade. I knew the building was getting old and unsafe but I saw a woman standing in the open doorway talking to a child and I thought about how fun it might be to walk over there and take a look.

[That old school burned to the ground many years ago. I think about it often which is probably why it popped up in my dream. It was a really neat building and it held a lot of really great memories for me.]

(If I was actually visiting my hometown and making an attempt to go inside a building that is no longer there, Don would be taking my measurements for a jacket with lots of buckles and extremely long sleeves!)

Dream: The final stop landed me at the post office where I worked for 13 1/2 years. There were several people in the office and everyone appeared to be incredibly focused on what they were doing without realizing I was even there. I walked back to the sorting case and received a rather eye opening shock! There was a mountain lion standing there!!!! I carefully turned around and walked quietly to the bathroom that was now located on the opposite end from where it was when I worked there. Once the door was closed, I pressed the button on the microphone that was attached to the headset I was wearing and informed everyone that there was, indeed, a mountain lion lurking around the sorting case!

[I had to think about the logic on this one but then I remembered how I played an April Fool's joke on one of my co-workers by telling her there was a mouse in the break room. She was as terrified as I would have been if it was a mountain lion and she immediately started thinking about how we were going to get rid of it. Her eyes were riveted to the spot the "mouse" was "hiding" and started discussing a list of people we needed to call. I wanted to hang onto the gag a little longer than I did but I really didn't want a bunch of people to receive phone calls about a hypothetical mouse!]

(If I ever really run across a mountain lion at work or anywhere for that matter, my first instinct would be to pet it and scratch it's chin and run my fingers down it's back to see if it's tail would pop up like the tails on domestic, pet variety cats but I'm betting something would stop me before I convinced myself petting, chin scratching and tail tests were a good idea.)

The next morning I jotted down a few notes to make next year's tax preparation a bit easier. I'm thinking morning or early afternoon will be a good time to work on this next year. I'm also having second thoughts about the significance of that mountain lion in my dream. He may have been the IRS. They do have similarities. They're both vicious when provoked, sneaky and unpredictable and why did that elderly lady mistake me for a Walmart employee? I wasn't wearing a maroon and gold satin robe and I distinctly remember leaving my big sequined hat in the car that day!

Ticked Off Tonsils

I'm getting sick. I haven't been sick for so long that I'm not sure if I remember how to do it. I do remember that I tend to get extremely impatient and I want to be better right away but doesn't everybody?

Several years ago I had a bout of tonsillitis that landed me an "all-expense paid by me" trip to a hospital room for three days in a row. I've had tonsillitis many times but I never got as sick with it as I did on this particular occasion. My tonsils were starting to feel a bit swollen so I made an appointment with my doctor. I was sent home with a bottle of pills and some encouraging words about how much better I was going to feel in a day or two. My tonsils had a rather different agenda. They began to swell and forgot to stop. I was only able to get down 2 doses of the antibiotics in pill form before my tonsils slammed the door shut to my esophagus. I called the clinic and said, "I think we need a different plan." It's a problem if you're not able to swallow your own saliva. Trust me. I could still breathe but I had to think about it and as long as I stayed calm and told myself I was going to be fine; I was fine....or as fine as you can be when you feel as if you've somehow gotten a tennis ball lodged in your throat. I'm sure the receptionist on the other end was a bit concerned when she heard my "tennis ball stuck in my throat" impersonation and it wasn't long before the doctor called me back with her plan. She went ahead and booked some rather expensive accommodations for me where they charge by the minute. I'm rather poor so I checked in and out each day until the prescribed plan of action was complete. The little antibiotic getaway was all inclusive so not only did I get to sit in my very own room with the vinyl recliner, but I also got fed....well, kind of. Every day they served the vein in my arm some delicious antibiotics in little clear bags but before the main course, they injected a dab of steroids as an appetizer. It was quite the party! It didn't take long for my tennis ball tonsils to realize the steroids had no plans of letting them continue to bounce around in the back of my throat. They made a rather quick turn in the right direction and I didn't feel sick again.....that is, until I got my bill for $1362! I sort of remember how little sleep I was getting before I got that sick. I also remember people saying, "You need to get more rest. You're going to get sick." I had no idea they were going to be right!

My sleep habits are much different now. I almost always get 6 or more hours of sleep per night. I am feeling incredibly drained and I have this little tickle in the back of my throat that is making me cough but I think I'll head to bed early and drink plenty of water and maybe, just maybe my tonsils won't decide to round up the rackets, set up the net and turn themselves into tennis balls again!

Embellishing The Ordinary

In general, I'm a pretty happy person. I suffer normal setbacks but I try not to let them consume me. Some people drag on rainy days. I sort of like a rainy day once in a while. They aren't as pleasant as the sunny variety but in my wild imagination, those are the times when the little pixies and fairies come out. Doesn't it always look like it has just rained when you see those kinds of pictures? Some of you are thinking, she's crazy but some of you are entering "pictures of fairies and pixies" into your search box and taking a look for yourself. For those of you that fear I've plummeted off the deep end, you will be glad to know I've never actually seen a pixie or a fairy. I'm just always prepared; in case I do.

I've always had a pretty colorful imagination and I can't say it's hindered any part of my life. It just embellishes the ordinary and makes my existence a bit more whimsical. I knew Santa wasn't "real" at a very young age but going along with this idea made it so much more fun. I was able to figure it out due to the fact that I watched Barnaby Jones, The Rockford Files and Quincy with my mom and I paid attention. As a result I became a bit of a detective and it didn't take long to realize the presents under my parents bed visible to anyone climbing the stairs backwards and peering under the railing surrounding the staircase were definitely not wrapped in any of the paper our gifts under the tree were wrapped in. The gifts "Santa" would leave for us were always wrapped with that paper I saw from my detective work and those boxes under my parents bed were always gone on the morning in question (Christmas Day). I never let on that I had figured out the technical aspects of the "Santa" theory and in my heart I will always believe that Santa is real. He's just not a flesh and blood person but rather a presence in my life that fills me with joy at the very mention of his name. He's right up there with the Easter Bunny and the Tooth Fairy and I'm quite sure their magic will always be a part of who I am.

My life isn't perfect and I'm perfectly okay with that. I like to encourage others to laugh more and stress less. I share a bit of my whimsy with almost everyone I meet and it's almost always accepted with open arms. I do occasionally run into those "stick in the mud" types but they don't bother me. I stuff them in the "It's not me, it's them" folder in my brain and then I pick up my hypothetical magic wand and move on with my day.

Smiley Smiled!

I worked the evening shift the other night and a woman that was given the nickname "Smiley" came in to shop. I'm not sure why, but she is showing up at the store several hours before we close now and she used to be the one that liked to show up a few minutes before closing time and insist on shopping for nearly an hour. This change in her time of arrival is exciting. She drives a lot of our employees bananas because she never smiles and she's a bit demanding but I sort of like her. She's unique and outspoken and those two qualities combined make for some very interesting conversations. There's no way of knowing what she is going to say next and I've learned that I need to practice keeping a straight face so that when she catches me off guard and my brain tells me to laugh I won't have to bite my lip as hard.

Tonight while I was measuring her fabric I almost called her Smiley. I'm not sure why my filter decided to save me, but it did. It's usually 100% in favor of me sticking my foot in my mouth but tonight was different. It heard my brain preparing a question for the customer in front of me and it quickly slipped in and grabbed that question and replaced it with "You've never told me your name. I see you quite a bit so I think it's time for me to know." Whew! That was a close one! She divulged a nickname first and after telling me it was a nickname I simply had to ask what her given name was. I told her they were both pretty names and it was then I received a tiny but noticeable smile. Progress.

It wasn't long before the conversation revealed the projects she planned to work on next. She was buying fleece to make her two cats blankets and one for herself. I told her I loved cats and before long I was looking at pictures of her beautiful babies. I learned quite a bit about them from her in a very short time. She stated the fact that her female is very prissy and feminine and loves to have her picture taken. I saw at least 43 shots of her taken with Smiley's phone and she does, indeed, look prissy and feminine. I also heard the story about how she acquired her male cat. I asked what his name was and when she announced it, I refused to make eye contact and my lip still hurts. This woman loves music and buys any fabric we have that features anything to do with music, be it radios, music notes, instruments....anything music related which explains why her cat's name is Mojo 107.5! Why not name your cat after your favorite radio station? I'm not sure why that tickled me but it did.

I guess it's safe to say I enjoyed my visit with Smiley tonight. She did absolutely nothing to ruffle any feathers. She didn't attempt to keep us open after closing time and she smiled....tonight, she actually smiled!

Page One

Had I followed through with all the plans I've had throughout my lifetime, I'd probably be more worn out than I am and no farther ahead. That comment may sound a bit pessimistic but in reality, it's just the truth. As I was cleaning my desk the other day I ran across a manila folder. I could tell by its weight that it didn't hold much and opening it revealed the very first page of the book I decided to write a few years ago. I'm not sure if you're ready for this but here is page one of my life story. I'm not sure why page two never followed but perhaps one day it will.

It was a hot July day back in 1965. A beautiful mother of two became a beautiful mother of three. Another daughter was added to this modest, hardworking family. I'm told I had lots of dark hair so the nurses were able to give me that Gerber baby look by rolling my hair into a little curl on the top of my head. Back then, women were kept in the hospital nearly a week after giving birth so the nurses had lots of time to play with babies and style their hair. I remember my mother telling me I was about as perfect as a baby could be. She has said this many times over the years but the initial thought was formed when she was under some pretty heavy medication. What followed in the years to come would prove, I wasn't in fact, perfect in any way, dang it.

My earliest memories stem back to the time I spent in the pen. It was a cage like structure and because there were absolutely no gymnastics "genes" in my "closet" I never once tried to escape. Not even once. You hear about kids jumping and climbing out of their cribs all the time. Not me. I set up camp and found things to do. I remember chewing the top of the nipples off my bottles. That was fun. You might say I designed one of the first "sippy" cups. Once the entire top of the nipple was removed, the contents flowed out quite easily but probably not as easy as it did when I figured out how to take the whole top off. Now that, that was interesting. I was a baby. Spilling stuff had no consequences. It was just fun so I did it a lot!

I also remember scribbling on the bedroom wall through the bars. My fingernail was my pencil and it worked great. The only drawback was the fact that it didn't have an eraser so once the canvas was full, this little budding artist would have to wait for mom and dad to move the crib to a new position. The bedroom was small so that didn't actually happen. Today, a house containing lead paint would most likely be condemned and

115

destroyed and the inhabitants would probably be sent to some research facility to study the effects of lead on the human brain. I'm 40 something and I'm still around and I can honestly say I haven't spent a lot of time trying to figure out if that is what caused me to be so odd. Wouldn't it be interesting if there was actually something good that stemmed from all of these materials that were determined to be unsafe? Okay, so I'm a dreamer too.

I suppose it was shortly after my third birthday, I spotted an interesting piece of property just outside my parent's bedroom door. That, I decided, would one day become my apartment. It was small but bigger than the place I was currently in. From where I saw it most often, I was pretty sure I could fit a couple of strollers, a doll crib and maybe even a Barbie townhouse in it. The possibilities seemed endless and it would be mine, all mine! I would no longer be bunking in my parent's room. What I didn't know then is that my "big bed" that followed the crib wasn't going to fit in my 48" x 64" apartment so I had to rent a bit of space in my sister's bedroom for my bed and learned that my apartment would be the place I would spend a lot of my day time hours. My sister wasn't thrilled but we made it work. Apparently I had trust issues with the new bed. The bars from the one I had grown quite accustomed to would always keep me from falling out. This new bed was downright scary. Subconsciously I would freak out while I was sleeping knowing that I could possibly be killed should I thrash about without my security bars to catch me! (The bed was approximately 24" high. A real dangerous situation, right?) I started to wet the bed and I can't really remember how often but I did it enough to still remember the feeling I had when I woke up. That is not a fond memory in itself but what amazed me most is how well my mother would handle it. I always returned at night to a nice, clean, dry bed. Not once do I remember her yelling at me nor did she ever make me feel bad in any way and eventually, I stopped. My mom was amazing.

Well, that's it. Page one. I'm sure page two will show up eventually as I did survive, much to my surprise.

A Riddle Ditty

Can you solve this riddle?

I'm betting there are no other statements in the world more true than the one I live by, laugh at and love. It's short and to the point. It eases stress if you believe it. It helps you laugh at yourself when you've really messed up and it's the key ingredient necessary if you ever want to savor the sweetness of unconditional love. Any ideas on what you think it might be?

Nobody is perfect.

This is the answer to my riddle.

We all make mistakes every day. We all have insecurities that can sometimes put distance between where we are and where we dream to be but it doesn't mean life can't be rewarding. One of my biggest insecurities is the fact that I've always been overweight. Excess weight is an insecurity that is pretty hard to hide. You carry it with you everywhere and sooner or later you will receive some very open opinions on what someone else thinks of this "obvious imperfection" they see before them. I've decided the people that take it upon themselves to educate you about your excessive weight have some of the lowest levels of self-esteem in existence. Think about it. The "declarers of the obvious" usually weigh less, at least mine have, and they almost appear to be afraid that you might see something they don't want you to see so by

117

getting a jab in first, they know they'll offend you and you'll walk away in shame.

I'll never forget two of the times when I was being mocked due to my excessive weight. One was back years ago when I was entering a store. There were two young guys in a car and they decided they should laugh and shout out some disturbing comments and honk the horn. I could have kept walking but I decided to try something just a bit different. I walked over to their car and offered my hand to them. They actually shook my hand. I proceeded to introduce myself. I've never seen two young men sit up so straight so fast in my life. They both looked so shocked and I'd be willing to bet their shorts were as full as their throats when it came time to say "hello" to me. I figured, if they want to mock and torment me, they might as well know just a little bit more about me and having to face me was most likely one of the hardest things they had ever done. I have no idea who they were but for some reason, I'll bet they never forgot me.

The second situation took place at a buffet type restaurant. There was a table with two young girls and a young guy. I was preparing to leave and they decided to throw some rather inconsiderate words my way. Little did they know I was the type that would stop dead in my tracks and head on over to their table and introduce myself. I'll never forget how their demeanor went from laughing hysterically to complete silence when they saw me coming. These introductions are always so much more uncomfortable for the hecklers than they have been for me. I don't think any of them realized what was about to happen and I'm betting they thought twice before tormenting someone again.

Like I said earlier, I don't honestly believe people that bully and torment others enjoy what they're doing as much as we might think. I believe it's their "suit of armor" that protects them from letting us see their insecurities. My dad would always say, "I'm no better than anyone else but I'm just as good." My mom has always said, "The only people that make mistakes are the ones that are actually doing something." I try to remember those words and do my best to live life to the fullest. I know I've hurt people. I know I've said some things I wish I could take back. Sometimes I misspell words while typing. Sometimes I forget to do something I know I shouldn't have forgotten to do. Sometimes I say the wrong thing. Sometimes I'm careless. But I'm human 100% of the time. I get out of bed every morning and try to put my best foot forward. It takes time to shower and do my hair and apply my makeup but I do it anyway. I'll never be a size 6 but over time I'm beginning to realize that I've never liked anyone for the size clothes they wear. I've been drawn in by intelligence, wit, charm, great senses of humor, warm hearts, protective natures but not once did I find myself determining who I was going to like best by how much they weighed. I just wish it hadn't taken almost 50 years to figure out I am perfectly imperfect right along with everybody else!

The whole point of this "riddle" is to help us remember that we're all human. We all have insecurities and we don't have to allow them to consume us. Let's confront our fears and open all those doors and windows to this exciting world we share and make the most of each and every day! Fat, skinny, short, tall, white, black, brown, yellow, red, rich or poor, we all matter and we're all unique in our very own fantastic way!

One Door With One Lock

I'm very thankful for public restrooms but you sort of have to wonder who designs some of those stalls that divide the toilets. I tend to gravitate towards the ones created for those with walkers or wheel chairs because they have more room. Most of the "regular" size ones have doors that open inward. I realize they do this so you don't whack people when you're coming out of them but I've been in several that have made me feel like the only way I'm getting out is if I'm willing to put one foot in the toilet! I've run into a few that have doors that literally touch the front of the throne when the door is swung inside. Is it just me or do you have issues with some of these situations?

A few things have changed for the better. I don't mind the toilets that flush themselves but I'm okay if they don't. I remember eating at a restaurant one time and upon visiting the restroom I saw a sign above the toilet that read, "Toilet will not flush automatically. Please push the button. We're very sorry for the inconvenience." I sort of chuckled in disbelief. Would there actually be people that would complain about that? I realize they wanted the toilets flushed and perhaps they figured people were growing accustomed to having the toilet flush itself but seriously, if it doesn't flush, are there really people that will just leave it? What am I saying? Of course there are!

I really like the new toilet paper dispensers I am seeing now that feature the "TP An Entire Block Of Houses" size rolls. They take a long time to run out and the paper rolls off pretty easy. I can still remember the regular size rolls of toilet paper they used to stock their restrooms with. It was thin enough to read a book through and tough enough to write a letter on and they would slide it onto those oval rollers that caused it to serve you several pieces of toilet paper, one square at a time. What were they thinking? Did they really want people sitting on those toilets for as long as it took to get enough to wipe? I've heard of pinching pennies but this was ridiculous.

The hand drying methods have changed too. It went from paper towels, to air dryers, to paper towels, to turbo air dryers and then back to paper towels with motion sensors. I sort of like the paper towel dispensers with motion sensors when they work. They seem pretty reliable but I've definitely had my share of times when I found myself waving at one of those crazy things every which way I could think of only to eventually notice the sign above it that says, "Out of order."

Now that we've discussed almost everything about a public restroom with several stalls it's time to share an experience I had a while back and in this particular restaurant there was only one restroom with one toilet and one door with one lock.

Every once in a while, before I moved, my friend and I would meet for supper. We always laughed and carried on like school girls and had the most wonderful time. We usually met at the same place and always joked that we would be there until they were ready to close but they sort of got used to us and they didn't seem to mind. On the night the lock issue transpired my friend had to leave a bit earlier than usual so we walked out to our cars together and eventually she left. I decided I should probably use the restroom before my 23 mile drive home so I went back inside the restaurant. It was a very nice, new facility and the unisex restroom was created by putting up some walls in this rectangular space with the door facing the dining area. I walked over to the bathroom door and pushed the lever handle down and began to push the door open. It gave me absolutely no resistance and once open my eyes caught site of the guy standing in front of the toilet taking care of his business, I almost let mine trickle down my leg!!! He tossed a pleasant smile my way and said, "I'm almost done and then it's all yours." What else could he say? He could see I was in shock. I'm not sure why but it felt almost as if time had stopped. I felt like I stood there for 20 minutes when in reality it was probably less than five seconds. Perhaps this guy forgot to lock the lock. Perhaps he thought he did but the lock was faulty or perhaps I was just one of his many victims and this type of thing gave him a thrill. I will most likely never know but from now on I plan to knock a few times before flying through any public unisex restroom doors that don't appear to be in use! Maybe those restrooms with those munchkins size stalls aren't so bad after all. I may have had a wet foot while trying to get out but my tinkle would have been in the toilet!

The Martha Macgyver Rescue!

Lawn mowers have given me a ton of grief but I suppose there were lessons learned so not all has been lost. When our grass trimming journey began over 20 years ago, we started out with several used Lawn Boy push mowers. All of them worked quite well except for the one that had a tire that would never stay on. I got so sick of putting it back on that I left it off one day and just kept mowing. Your lawn takes on a very interesting look when you do this. I don't recommend it. That bad boy was eventually replaced by a brand new discount store model. It arrived in a box and required assembly. I am all about reading instructions but it seems a rather anxious man decided instructions were for idiots and before I knew it, he had the mower assembled and it was on its way out the door to receive its first taste of gasoline and the chance to show us what it could do. Not long after the engine fired up I heard it shut off. I met someone coming up the steps to inform me that two of the wheels had fallen off and the other two were wobbling. In the instructions I began reading when the box was first opened, I remembered seeing something about the direction the curved washers needed to face when attaching the tires to the frame. The curved washers that were no longer attached to the frame. The curved washers lost in the grass that were now patiently waiting for Martha Macgyver to arrive! I pondered for a bit and due to the fact that I am a "Martha Stewart/Macgyver" type I decided to create a metal detector with my magnetic pin cushion duct taped to the end of the broom handle. I remember someone telling me this was a crazy idea...crazy until he heard the first curved washer "clink" when it hit the magnet. Eventually all the missing parts were recovered and the mowing commenced.

A few years down the road the large yard began to convince our tired feet that a riding lawn mower might be nice. We located a used riding lawn mower at a reasonable price and hoped it would give us several years of worry free lawn maintenance. It made several attempts to serve us well but it had a very warped sense of humor. It loved to untie it's rope so when you pulled it, in an attempt to start the engine, it would come completely out and at record speed. That was an unpleasant surprise every time but the mower enjoyed it so much it "pulled" that trick more than it should have. There was a certain way you had to wind the rope back on the pulley and every time it came loose I would call my dad and ask him to tell me, yet again, which way I had to wind it. It also liked to lose air in its tires and if you ever mow with a low tire on a rider you get the very same look as when you mow your lawn with a 3 wheeled push mower. Once again, I don't recommend it. I suppose we got sort of used to the hi-jinks but the day I heard the sonic boom coming from a cloud of smoke in the back yard, I knew only one would be coming out of that cloud alive and I was pretty sure it wasn't going to be the lawn mower. Upon seeing a rather bewildered man walking away from the wreckage I knew I would be rearranging an already strained budget to include a payment on a new lawn mower. Things worked out fine and before long we had a new rider sitting beside the old one.

I didn't spend a lot of time wondering what to do with the old rider but one day, while I was putting clothes in the dryer the phone rang. It was my dad. He asked if we wanted to sell our old blown up mower. I was shocked and said, "Are you kidding me? Who would want it?" He had a friend that had an engine but no mower and due to the fact that we had a mower with a blown engine, he thought maybe we would want to sell it. I said we would and then asked him how much he thought it was worth. He sold mowers like this for years but said he had no idea and then handed the phone to his friend. I was immediately asked what we wanted for it and I said, "I have no idea. Make me an offer." He said, "How about $350?" I felt myself gazing at the bubble that had formed over my head showing me clips from all the tormenting times that mower had given us and I said, "How about $300?" He said, "SOLD!"

It's not every day you make someone an offer and they come back with a counter offer that is less but all I could think about is what a nightmare that mower had been and how bad I felt about taking someone's money for something that caused us a ton of grief! Trust me, I took a lot of grief about my wheeling and dealing skills but you can't say I'm not a conscientious saleswoman!!! I guess it's good I've never had an overwhelming desire to sell cars.

Temptation & Forgiveness

Having a baby sister is probably one of the worst things that ever happened to my sister and brother. They both agree I was spoiled and got out of doing a lot of dirty work because I was the baby. I'm not sure if they've ever thought about the fact that I didn't choose our birth order. It just happened and there was nothing any of us could do to change it.

Holding the youngest spot wasn't glamorous all the time. I don't remember my brother or sister reminiscing about the "spit" baths mom used to give them. I love my mother but being bathed in her spit was something I wish I could forget. I don't remember them saying they got their chubby little cheeks pinched a gazillion times followed by several thousand pinches on their arms due to the fact that they were just so darn soft. I don't remember them having bouts of uncontrollable blushing when they were in high school when they were introduced to people as their mother's baby. All of these things happened to me and very early on I decided I had two choices. I could let it consume me and turn me into what felt like one of those furry little monkeys on a stick you dream of buying at the circus or I could learn to just embrace my existence and be thankful I had a mother that loved me as much as she did and still does.

I must say my circumstances definitely contributed to the early development of a very good sense of humor. It came in very handy. I used it when I got bored. I used it when I knew I was getting the best of my siblings and I often used it instead of crying when appropriate. I learned rather quickly that it was a bit more effective than crying when attempting to diffuse volatile situations I found myself wandering into. I did try crying first a number of times before switching to the "laughter" approach. I'm not sure why older siblings find it necessary to have some sort of control over the baby but mine did and the only thing they accomplished was teaching me that it was okay to give into temptation. Below is an example of that irresistible temptation I gave in to.

For some reason my sister would never let me sit on her bed. (I'm betting you can see how this is going to play out.) When she was gone and I knew she was gone, I would walk across our bedroom floor, stop when I reached her bed, turn myself around and sit. I'm not sure what I expected but no music played, no stuffed animals came to life, no glitter fell from the ceiling but temptation got an early grip on me and there I sat. I'm not sure how, but she could always tell when I did this and when she yelled at me, it was then, I learned to laugh. One would think this would ignite more intense anger but it actually didn't. It didn't until the day I chose to call my sister something I heard on Saturday Night Live. Dan Aykroyd and Jane Curtain would do a news bit and Dan would repeatedly call Jane a name consisting of two words. I was probably 12 at the time and quite naive and I had no idea what it meant but the audience would always laugh. I decided it had to be pretty hilarious so one day I decided to do a little Dan Aykroyd impersonation. I was prepared to share a ton of laughter with my sister and it was then and only then, I called her an "ignorant slut." It was obvious, she knew what this meant. Time slipped into slow motion. There was no laughter. I don't think I found out that day what it meant but I found out it didn't pertain to my sister and the fact that she let me live still remains a mystery.

Little sisters mean well. Little sisters torment their older siblings but when little sisters grow up, they realize just how blessed they are to have a big sister and big brother to love.

The Little Hammers

As I near the ripe old age of 50, my body has decided to send me some rather interesting messages. I'm never sure when the hands of fate will deliver them so I've learned that I need to be prepared 100% of the time. In my 20's you never would have found a full size bottle of both Excedrin Migraine and Ibuprofen in my purse. In my 20's you wouldn't have seen me holding anything with small print as far away from my eyes as my arms could reach just so I could see the small stinking print that is way smaller than it used to be. In my 20's you wouldn't have run across my rather impressive collection of magnifying glasses and you wouldn't have noticed the silver sparkle that has decided to illuminate my hair. I've heard people say they would do things a lot different if they had the chance to start over but I don't think I would. Everything I've experienced has taught me something. It's unfortunate to a point, I suppose, but the bad experiences have taught me the most.

In almost 50 years there are lots of things I've learned that have benefited me tremendously but the one I treasure most is the one that taught me God's plan was just a tad bit different than mine. I had no desire to go to college. I had no desire to pursue any type of professional career. I wanted to be wife and mother. I practiced being a mom for years. I drove my parents crazy because all I ever wanted for my birthday or for Christmas was, as my dad would put it, another dang doll! God knew this but He had a slightly different plan. It wasn't an easy one to grasp and there were times I really wanted a better answer to my "whys" but I can't say I'd change the way things turned out.

I wasn't able to give birth or experience motherhood first hand. During the years of trying to make this happen, all nine of them, I cried more than I thought a person could cry. I found out what depression was. I found out what acceptance was but in the process a rather hard shell formed around my heart when it came to children. It was my way of protecting something that had already ached more than I believed it should have ever had to. I had no idea fate had plans of removing that shell nor did I know how it would go about it. All I knew was I had to endure a very painful divorce, move back home and get a job working a ton of hours while trying to sort out all the things that went wrong over the course of twenty years. It was then fate began knocking down that very hard shell by using the warmth and love of some very amazing children I would see every day at the convenience store where I worked. Their school bus stopped there to pick them up but we always had time to visit before they left for the day. I had no idea what was happening but eventually I found myself bonding with some of the kindest and most beautiful young people on the face of this earth. We would gather around the till and talk about all the exciting things that were happening in their lives. Sometimes I would bring treats and offer advice when someone was being picked on or not feeling the best.

There was one young girl that divulged how scared she was walking those two blocks to the store every morning because it was dark outside. I remember being scared of the dark and I would never have wanted to walk by myself in the dark for two blocks when I was her age so I had a little chat with her dad after she left. He shrugged it off as her being silly but he did start giving her a ride after that. She thanked me.

One little first grade girl always had a way of tickling me with her innocence and I still enjoy those memories. One day she was standing near the till when an adult was checking out. The pen holder on the counter was empty again and I said, "I can't believe how many pens grow legs and walk right out that door!" She pondered for a bit and then in a very serious way she said, "Do the pens really grow legs and walk out of here?"

Three young kids that had been staying at their grandparent's house over the weekend came bursting in the door one morning, all excited to tell me their grandpa and grandma's cat had her kittens! I asked how they knew and they said, "Well, because she doesn't look like a soccer ball this morning!" I would venture to say mama cat was most likely black and white. Wouldn't you?

I also had the chance to go to movies with some of them and take some of them out for supper and there was one, in particular, that owns the most pieces of that shell I wore around my heart. She chose to spend as much of her free time with me as she could, even when I was in a bad mood. Often times I would ask her why she liked me even when I was crabby and she would always say, "Because you're Bev." How many adults would say that? She is more precious than some of the people in her life will ever realize or give her credit for. She's resilient. She's beautiful inside and out and mature beyond her years but that doesn't mean she won't make wire loops and homemade bubble solution with me so I can look less silly when I want to be amazed by bubbles. I'm thinking she would even be okay with me telling people it was her idea!

One evening she and I were visiting and on the way to her house we drove past a lot where a house had burned a few years ago. She said her friend told her she was in that house when it started on fire. I said, "Really?" And then she said, "No, she wasn't and I didn't believe her anyway." I asked why not and she said, "She also told me she was a mermaid." You've got to love a kid blessed with a healthy dose of common sense!

Another night my sister, my little sidekick and I went to the taco feed down the street. They ran out of taco meat right after we got our first tacos assembled which meant no second taco and it was almost as cold inside as it was outside but then, out of the blue, a particularly fascinating four year old decided to have a little chat with me. She is as whimsical as the day is long and I've learned that if I just talk to her without a lot of facial expressions and rather low key, I will get responses that blow my mind. She decided we should plan a shopping trip together and asked me to write a list of things we needed. Headbands, tiaras, and pink dresses were going to be necessities. I threw in the idea that we should probably pick up a camel and maybe a monkey and some banana flavored nail polish which were fine but she was a bit apprehensive about the hedgehog idea. Her mother came over and asked what she was up to. I explained that we were planning a shopping trip. She asked where we were headed. I said, "Tim-buck-two and my little friends' whole face lit up and she said, "YESSSSS!" Apparently she had heard of the place but had not actually shopped there. During this visit I was able to forget that having another taco might have been fun and that when a four year old warms your heart you feel warm all over!

I feel sort of bad that I allowed that shell to form around my heart all those years ago but time has shown me that it wasn't something I needed to hang onto forever. The little "hammers" that broke that shell into pieces exposed a loving heart that was always there and helped it to realize being a "mom" isn't just about giving birth. It's about caring and listening and being there for those precious little people that are so willing to share their time and give you their love.

The Fly Did Not Survive

Do you worry about things? Have you ever allowed yourself to be so consumed by worry that you actually shortened the time you could have actually been enjoying something?

Personally, I think we all have things that bother us from time to time and worrying about the outcome just usually happens. I've heard worrying is our way of telling God how to run the world. I've also heard that worrying causes insomnia, anxiety, high blood pressure, ulcers and acid reflux, heart palpitations and several other nasty things. I'm not sure why we do this. It doesn't change the outcome or fix anything. It just makes us miserable mentally and physically if we're good at it but if you're like me, it feels rather involuntary.

Yesterday while Don and I were out for a drive, I saw the calculator in my purse and it sparked a memory from my childhood. It's a story about why not to worry. It taught me a valuable lesson and helped me to realize there are some things I just need to enjoy while I can.

I was probably 10 years old. I remember spying the tiny little package under the Christmas tree that had my name on it. I had no idea what it could be but when December 25th finally arrived I found out the colorful paper had been hiding a brand new calculator complete with its very own faux leather "protective" pouch! It featured a brushed silver finish surrounding shiny silver keys and an illuminated greenish yellow digital display screen. It was sleet and sophisticated and it could add, subtract, multiply and divide like you wouldn't believe! I was in my glory with this amazing tool. I was in my glory until the worry of a dead battery began to consume me. I grew up in a tiny little town so stores that sold calculator batteries and the money it took to buy them weren't plentiful. I knew the only way to keep things working would be to use the calculator as little as possible which would save on the battery. The excitement of having this amazing tool was still there but I knew I needed to limit my usage so that is what I did. I remember asking my dad where a person would buy new batteries for it and he yelled out, "If they're not dead yet, don't worry about it!" Oh how I wish I had listened.

Spring arrived and my bike was in dire need of a stroll down the road. Every year it took a while before you got your butt broke in to that bike seat so I decided my first trip would take me across town to my grandma and grandpa's house. It would give me a chance to rest my butt on one of their dining room chairs before returning home and it would also give me a chance to show off my shiny silver calculator! It was small so I slipped it in its faux leather case and off we went. I arrived at my destination and as kids often do, I blurted out the reason for my visit and then proceeded with a demonstration that showed grandma and grandpa all the cool things this amazing calculator had up it's "sleeve." My grandpa commented on the cool lighted greenish yellow display panel and seemed quite impressed with my little helper. After a bit I snapped the power button into the "off" position and returned the calculator to its "protective" sleeve. We continued visiting and eventually my grandpa spotted a fly buzzing around the room. He asked me to hand him his fly swatter that was hanging on a nail near my seat. I took it down and as I was handing it to him I realized it was definitely homemade. It had a rather heavy gauge wire forming the handle and a piece of thick black rubber attached to the end. It wasn't a design that was ready for the production line but you could tell it was definitely not going to have any trouble eliminating anything it came into contact with.

I'm not sure how one fly can create such a raucous but they can and the one buzzing around our heads did. It would land and then take off and land again. My grandpa was getting so frustrated so I started visiting with my grandma about something and before long I forgot all about "the hunt" going on. That is....until.....the fly landed on.....you guessed it, my faux leather calculator case that was holding my precious calculator!!!! My grandpa swooped in and before I could stop what was about to happen....WHAMMMMMM! The fly did not survive. I reluctantly slid the device out of its case and it wasn't looking good. The beautiful greenish yellow lighted display window was shattered. I was shattered. It was possible the calculator might still be able to do its job but without a screen to display it's answers, it was useless.

Obviously, I survived and it gave me a chance to think about all the fun I could have had with that calculator had I not been worrying about how I would replace the battery. I learned that life is meant to be lived and enjoyed. We shouldn't wait for circumstances to be perfect. We shouldn't worry. Worrying doesn't benefit our lives in any way. It holds us back and forces us to believe it's in control. I can't say I never worry anymore but I am trying to worry only if I can't find anything better to do and that seems to be working out quite well!

A Chair By The Door

Have you ever stopped to think about all the things mice must see when they situate themselves in corners?

I was telling a co-worker about a shopping adventure that transpired this past weekend and I caught myself saying, "I would have loved to have been a mouse in the corner when my husband and our neighbor, Sam, went chair shopping on Saturday." I decided it was write worthy so here goes.

Last week Don was out of town for work. Our current home is quite small and he has asked me to agree, on numerous occasions, not to bring anything more into this already cramped space and to simply wait until we move to a bigger house. I try to agree with him but great deals weaken me and last week a great deal presented itself. Before I succumbed I decided I needed to talk it over with Don. I've been the one attempting to enforce communication and this was definitely a communication issue. The great deal was a really nice pressed back oak chair at one of the local thrift stores I frequent on a regular basis. I thought it would look nice sitting where the green plastic lawn chair was near our door where we sit to put on our shoes. Don didn't really have a problem with the lawn chair but now that his bachelor pad became our home, it had to go! The asking price on the chair I spotted was $24.99. I found the same chair on the internet for $139.99. This, my friends, was a great deal! I broke the news to Don in a text and he asked me to send a picture. His response was positive so I got ready and headed to the store. I walked around for a few minutes so as not to appear too uncontrollably excited but eventually I wandered down the aisle where the chair was sitting the day before and it.....was......GONE!! The approval period lasted too long and I lost out. I was bummed but it wouldn't be the first time and I knew life would go on. I really thought this was the end of the story. I was wrong.

I had visited with our friend Sam about the chair I wanted and Don knew about it and they both knew I didn't get it. Here is what transpired.

On Saturday, while I was at work, Don decided to do a little shopping. When I got home from work he met me at the door and as I entered the house I saw a brand new, very attractive chair occupying the space where the plastic green lawn chair had been sitting!

He pointed out some minor flaws it had on the back but they weren't at all visible from where it's sitting and then he asked me to guess how much it cost. About then I saw Sam sitting in the dining room and they both kept saying "no, lower" every time I guessed the price. They found it at a rather well known furniture store and it is really nice so I started my guesses at $139. From there I went to $129, $100, $79, $59 and it wasn't until I got to $19.99 that Don said, "It cost $25 bucks plus tax!" Apparently they went to this store and looked around. They spotted the chair and it was marked $59. Don said he didn't want it for that price as it was damaged but Sam said, "Ask them if they'll take less." Don didn't want to so Sam did. The sales clerk said she would have to ask her manager and when she returned the guys were told it was a go for $25! Sam followed her up to the counter to pay for the chair and then told her he would like to finance the purchase and offered to pay $5 per month. Apparently they all got a pretty good chuckle out of it and the chair is now being used daily and making the area near our door look mighty fine!

I'll bet you would have liked to have been "a mouse in the corner" right along with me when those two characters set out to create a happy ending to "the chair by the door" story!

The Mint Green Surprise

Don's work schedule can get a bit hectic at times and it's not uncommon for him to be gone several nights a week. He gets sort of used to living out of a suitcase but packing it is always a chore and he appreciates anything I'm willing to do to help so once I found out he was planning to be on the road again I began to assemble several of the things I knew he would be needing as I had some time before work. Due to the fact that he loves the way I get his shirts suitcase ready, I gathered as many as I could find and got them all neatly folded. Next I walked around the bed and decided to see what was still in his suitcase from the last time he was away. I wanted to give him a bit of a jump start on packing and removing the things still in there from the last trip seemed like a pretty logical idea. At first all I noticed were some assorted t-shirts and a pair of jeans and a work shirt but then I noticed something odd. It wasn't a color I was used to seeing when I opened Don's suitcase so my hands immediately took hold of the item and I must say, what I saw was just a bit different than what I was expecting and it didn't take long to realize the very feminine mint green pajamas trimmed in matching lace WEREN'T MINE!

What a way to start your day!

It's funny how your brain immediately thinks the worst but then feels guilty and makes a very immediate attempt to save your man's rear end? It comes up with an impressive assortment of logical reasons your man has women's pajamas in his suitcase that don't belong to you. Below is a list of what transpired within the amount of time it took me to take hold of them and head down the hall for the photo shoot about to happen that would be followed by a text explaining to him what I had found.

1. I have Alzheimer's and these pajamas are actually mine and I just forgot.

2. They really aren't there. They are simply a figment of my imagination. (This one had flaws from the get-go. I had the item in question in my hand for crying out loud!)

3. The neighbor is quite the joker and I'll bet he planted them in that suitcase when we weren't looking, just to spice things up in our relationship.

4. They're a gift for me he found at a thrift store because it was obvious they had definitely been worn a few times and when he saw them he just knew I'd love them so he bought them and forgot to give them to me.

5. He's a cross dresser. Oh shit. (At this point I was glad I had located my phone for the picture I was planning on taking to send to Don. I have nothing against cross dressers but we just don't have the closet space for more clothes!) (Okay, I'm lying. I don't want to deal with a cross dresser.)

And then I remembered the last hotel he stayed at wasn't a hotel at all but rather the spare bedroom at his parent's house. After a rather long "ulcer inducing" wait time following my "It's no biggie. I was just surprised." text to him, I found out what had happened. He saw them laying in the chair in the bedroom while staying at his parent's house a few weeks ago and thought they were probably mine. He wasn't sure how they ended up in his suitcase but we did learn that his mom was the one who put them in the spare bedroom thinking they were mine. She and he and I still don't know who lost their pajamas but we do know they weren't a figment of my imagination and they had nothing to do with number 6 on the list of thoughts I had racing through my head! Thank goodness!

(No, I didn't actually type number 6. I think you can figure it out!)

A follow-up from the day after the "Mint Green Surprise."

Don and I didn't get a chance to talk until the next day due to our opposite work schedules but what transpired when he got off work was quite interesting.

First he called his mother and asked her if she realized those pajamas she put in the spare bedroom nearly gave me a heart attack. I also found out she was the one that had actually put them in her son's suitcase so he wouldn't forget to take them.

Next the "joker" neighbor popped over while I was still at work and gave Don a rather impressive selection of ways to handle this situation. Don overruled all of them due to the fact that Sam has not had a girlfriend for as long as we've known him and also because Don knew his woman didn't need any more fuel added to the ulcer that had already burned up the walls of her stomach before traveling on to her intestines!

I love happy endings.....don't you?

Monday Hates Me

My existence was much less hectic today. Yesterday had several flaws. It started bad and ended weird and all I can say is Monday hates me.

Due to the fact that it was the anniversary date of my dad's death, it got off to a somewhat emotional start. Once Don headed off to work I decided to get his packing started for a work trip and found some women's pajamas in his suitcase from his last work trip that weren't mine. I went to work and while at the registers, I rang up a sale and entered "cash" as the payment method instead of "check" and during my attempt to fix this blunder the register locked up and forced me to sweet talk the very patient and kind customer into sticking around for just a few more minutes. Later on I got locked out of the management access to some of the programs needed to finish a number of end of day tasks which translated very poorly in my already overwhelmed and depressed brain. Monday left me feeling as if the sky, was indeed falling and there was nothing I could do to stop it.

Today I woke up fearing I would be attempting to remove all the rumble on top of me when the sky fell but much to my amazement, the sky was just where Monday left it. Another thing that impressed me is something Annie has said for years, "The sun will come out tomorrow!" and it did. Don was able to convince me I didn't have Alzheimer's, that he never shops for me at thrift stores, that he isn't a cross dresser and that he definitely thought those darn mint green pajamas were mine and I got my management access back after one very quick call to Matt in Systems Support. I ended up having a very nice conversation with a customer too as she searched for her fabric coupons. I had to help her just a bit and then said, "Our store loves for you to save money. We're sort of like the Hokey Pokey....saving you money, that's what we're all about!" The laughter that rolled out of that woman was enough to loosen the snow caps on the mountains in Alaska! Had I tried a line like that yesterday I would have probably gotten beat with a shopping bag and ran over with the cart! What a difference a day can sometimes make! Tuesday, you are my friend!

The "Bar-beer" Shoppe

Sunday night Don showered and then asked if I would give him a haircut. I obliged and before I was finished our neighbor stopped in. He could see I was doing a pretty impressive job on Don's hair so he said something about me cutting his hair next. I told him I would and could so that was that. He was next on the schedule. Each of the guys were having a beer and I said maybe I should start a "Bar-beer Shoppe." It might be more enjoyable for the customers and if the scissors slipped once in a while, the ears would tend to be a bit less sensitive....oh yes, my wheels were turning.

Once Don's excess hair had taken up residence inside the vacuum, it was Sam's turn. He asked for a buzz cut with a No. 3 attachment on the clipper. Don has a ton of clippers so I knew it wouldn't be hard to find the proper equipment. After scrounging around for a bit I found a clipper and Don found a No. 3 attachment for it and off I went to set sail on Sam's head of unsuspecting hair. Things were rolling along pretty smooth and I remember joking about how terrible it would be if the cordless clipper died half way through the cut and then, the cordless trimmer died half way through the cut!!! Sam went racing to the bathroom to see how ridiculous he looked. At this point I jotted down a mental note on my mental list to keep customers away from mirrors until their haircut is finished. I also added that I should make sure all rechargeable trimmers are fully charged before starting a haircut . I felt this was something I would need to know when I started my business.

Eventually he came back and we decided the clipper would be fully recharged in less than 30 minutes so all three of us started watching TV. I tried not to look at Mr. Half-A-Haircut because I never like it when somebody laughs at me and I feared I might laugh and that just wouldn't be very nice. Thirty minutes later I went over and unplugged the trimmer and was totally shocked when it didn't fire up AT ALL!!!! Sam freaked out and about then Don hopped off the couch and found another trimmer with a No. 2 attachment. I reassured Sam it would work just fine and that the No.2 hairs would blend right in with the No. 3 hairs. It wasn't long before I knew this statement would become a bold face lie. I immediately removed the No. 2 trimmer from my hand which caused a bit of panic in Sam but I was able to keep him on the chair and just then Don showed up with yet another trimmer with yet another No. 3 blade attachment. I finished the haircut and all of the blood pressures that had risen slightly to more than slightly to almost a HEART ATTACK returned to normal and everyone was happy. Sam got out his wallet and was going to pay me for the mental torture he had just endured and I said, "Let's just say your first haircut was complimentary!" You've got to love a guy that offers to pay money for a haircut that nearly gave him a heart attack!

"New & Improved"

As I was getting ready for work this morning I got to thinking about the mascara I had recently purchased. I remember scanning at least 8 or 10 different ones before I made my selection and what I determined is that all of them are basically designed to do the very same thing. The packaging might suggest that one will lengthen your lashes while another will thicken them and yet another claims that it contains a miraculous component that will actually help you to grow longer, thicker lashes of your very own! A statement like that almost matches the excitement my friend and I got when we were 7 years old and we managed to scrounge up enough money to send away for the seeds to grow our very own family of sea monkeys!!!

The monkeys and the mascara got me thinking about the terminology marketing strategists use to excite us and create a feeling of need for the all the products they continue to send off to manufacturers that eventually fill warehouses and store shelves we browse every time we run out of something. I'm not sure I will ever understand the idea behind approximately 37 assorted mascaras or 130 different kinds of shampoo or several different styles of "zippers" on zip-loc bags nor will I ever fully comprehend the rather large selection of toilet paper. Have you ever thought about the end result of your toilet paper purchase? It's something you will never see again once it's used so I sometimes find myself wondering if flowers embossed on it are all that necessary and does it really have to be as thick as the fabric you would use to reupholster your couch? There is one brand I've seen that literally feels like thick, high quality flannel and I have often times entertained the idea of making something out of it rather than clean my under carriage and watch it swirl its way into the great beyond!

As far as all of the mechanical things we use, whether it's an appliance or tool of some kind, I'm sure you've noticed there is almost nothing "built to last" anymore. The part of this I find so contradictory is that we are encouraged to make our environment more "green" and there is a lot of recycling happening but I've also heard people say it's cheaper to buy a new printer rather than purchase ink cartridges for the printer they already have. Am I the only one that finds this rather odd?

I figured out quite some time ago that we should all steer clear of anything that states it's "New and Improved!" For starters, if it's new, it can't be improved upon yet. If it's an old product they have decided to re-invent, they should not be using the word "New." When this happens "New" is code for "Let's convince our customers to pay more for less!" What they don't want you to notice is that they've reduced the size of the box or packaging so less of the same great product fits in it and then they offer it to you at a "New" low price for a limited time. What they don't tell you is that the "New" low price is the old price you were paying for the product that used to come in a bigger box or larger package. "Improved" is a word that should never be used to sell products that have been on the market for years. "Improved" is code for "We've found a way to create the products you have used for years and dearly love with materials that cost us a lot less so we can charge you more because we've made it clear that we've improved it which will convince you it's going to work better when in fact it's going to be a total and complete waste of your hard earned money."

I suppose there is really nothing we can do to change the way our products are created or re-created. It's something that has gone on for years and the chances of it changing are almost as likely as the chances of having your Sea Monkeys look anything like they did on the advertisement you saw posted in the magazine that convinced you to order. Afterall, that advertising was created by a marketing strategist that would eventually have grandchildren doing as good of a job as he did back in the day!

A "Cheeseburger" Payment Option

I'm sure you've had experiences that will most likely stay with you for the rest of your life. As I grow older, I've noticed my memory isn't what it was when I was in my 20's but my niece said something last night that tickled me and I am quite certain this is one that is going to stay with me for a very long time. I must share.

My niece Andrea, her husband Shawn and I were having a conversation when my other niece, Allison, walked up and started rubbing Andrea's back. When she walked away Andrea said, "When Shawn rubs my back he always asks what I plan to do for him and I usually say, let me think about it." There was a short pause and then she said, "Sometimes I get him a cheeseburger."

I am not sure why that struck me so funny but it did. Not long after that conversation another one got started with Allison. I ended up telling her about the "cheeseburger" payment option for back rubs which she enjoyed and together we had another great laugh.

As I was getting ready to leave the party we had all gathered together for, I noticed my niece, April, rubbing Allison's back and as I was walking out the door I made eye contact with Allison and said, "I'm not 100% sure but you might owe her a cheeseburger....just sayin!" And we laughed again!

Now, I have no idea who was president when the astronauts landed on the moon and I no longer have the words memorized to the Gettysburg Address but I do love to laugh and I can say with confidence that I will never forget there are people in this world that accept cheeseburgers as payments for back rubs and they are my kind of people!!!

Oops! That Wasn't For You

I'm beginning to believe gadgets and my age are a lethal combination! A few months ago I got a new cell phone. I drug my feet just a bit as my old one was still working just fine and we got along really well. Getting a new one would mean I would have to learn a bunch of new stuff and quite frankly, I didn't want to learn a bunch of new stuff. The older I get the less fond I am of deciphering all the techie terms used in instruction manuals and the video tutorials tend to go on and on and on and lose me somewhere before they're finished and I find that I'm no farther ahead than before I started.

The new phone is pretty nice and it has been taking it pretty easy on me but I have noticed one tiny little glitch and that tiny little glitch has caught me off guard three times now in the past five days. When you tap on the little white envelope on the main screen it will open to the last person you texted unless you remember to hit the back button after that communication is complete. I don't always remember this and I send the most texts to Don so when it opens, I always override the possibility of the text going to someone else and start typing away. On Friday I sent "Can I trade you a hundred for 2 fifty's?" to my niece. She didn't respond. I'm not surprised. I wouldn't have either. Who would ask that question just out of the blue? On Saturday I sent a picture of myself with puckered lips and the word "Smootch!" to my sister and today I sent "How does being home feel baby?" to my brother! I realize this isn't the end of the world and I know I need to pay better attention to who I'm sending what to but after 3 goofs in 5 days, it's probably safe to say there will be a lot more unsuspecting recipients of random texts before I get my brain retrained!

I remember a similar "non-cell phone related" situation a few years ago when I was still working at the C-store. It was a Saturday morning and Don was there for the weekend and while I worked he decided to do a bit of tree trimming in my mom's yard. When he had his trailer full of branches he would drive by the C-store en route to the city dump and he would honk to let me know he was going by. I ended up sitting by the desk doing a bit of paperwork and I heard a pickup pull in and park right by the window. I glanced out and saw a silver vehicle and decided Don must have needed a break and so when the door opened, I belted out a "Hey Baby! How's it going?" before turning around. There was no immediate response so I whirled around in the desk chair to investigate and the guy that walked in the door wasn't Don! We were both shocked and I said, "You're not my baby!" It's so hard to know what to say after something like that. The unsuspecting guy was very nice and made every attempt to keep the conversation rolling about anything and everything that had nothing to do with the greeting he received when he walked in the door! You sort of hope incidents like that are few and far between and mine were.....that is until I got a new cell phone and forgot to "look" before I "leaped!"

After The Beep

I'm a bit old fashioned, I suppose, so when I moved to the big city I wanted a land line telephone. Don and I both have cell phones but the new cable/internet provider we chose to use offered us a plan that included a land line with a voice mailbox. We don't use it all that often but we've sure gotten a lot of interesting messages and to date, none of them have been for us!

For a while, every time I checked the messages, they were for Evelyn. Apparently her lawyer's office was trying to get a hold of her and for some reason, they kept calling our number. I don't check the messages every day and I probably should but the day I finally did, there were at least four messages and each revealed a rather desperate attempt to reach Evelyn. I decided I should probably call the people leaving the messages and let them know they had the wrong number for their client and that is why she wasn't calling them back. I learned several interesting things when calling a "call back" number when you aren't Evelyn. For starters, they have a rather unfriendly tone. It sort of sounds like the tone you would expect to hear if you had just told them you were calling from the auditing department at the IRS. It's rather evasive but they keep listening to you even though they don't want to believe you because believing you would determine they had made a mistake. Eventually they thank you and with the same puzzled sounding voice used for all of their responses, they hang up the phone and sit at their desk for a minute trying to decide what to do next.

I am happy to report the calls for Evelyn finally stopped but today Don said, "Bev, do you realize there are 8 messages on the phone? You should go through them and get at least some of them deleted." I asked him why he didn't just delete them and he said, "None of them are for me." I followed that comment with a rather confident, "Well, I'm betting none of them are for me either."

What happened next would reveal we were both correct. Five of the eight messages stored on our phone were from Mary in California and she was planning a trip to ND and was wondering if her dear old friend Arlene would mind if she stayed for a few days. Like I said before, I don't listen to these messages every day so by the time phone messages number 4 and 5 had arrived, Mary was ready to end her friendship with good old Arlene and tell Arlene to take a flying leap to Hell!

Don heard the messages too and we both decided we better give Mary a call. The fate of her friendship with Arlene was at stake!

I dialed the number and after 3 short rings Mary was on the other end. I said, "Hello Mary. My name is Beverly and I just wanted to let you know that the number you've been calling in an attempt to reach Arlene was in fact, the wrong number." She had that same unfriendly tone and her first question was, "Who is this?" I explained again that she had the wrong number for good old Arlene and then after a brief pause she burst into laughter and said, "Now that's good old ND for ya! I miss ND! I'm coming for a visit soon and I realized I had the wrong number for Arlene and I was able to get in contact with her." She sounded like a wonderful woman and she has our number so if she gets bored while she's here maybe she'll decide to give us a call!

These situations made me think about the Christmas card I sent to the wrong Neil and Julie this past season. The Neil and Julie we know are Don's cousins and I didn't have their address but I knew what city they lived in, or so I thought, so I just Googled it and about a month after sending the card we got it back along with a wonderful letter and picture of the family that received it. They scratched and scratched and scratched their heads but neither of them could place us! I plan to write back to them and let them know that they really don't know us so that they can finally have a bit of closure from their mystery Christmas card. I wonder if they know Evelyn or Arlene. I might mention those names in the letter just for fun!

This Did Not Just Happen

Several years ago, I was hired by a local hotel to work the night shift. I have always been a "night person" so I thought this job would work out great. It was sort of weird going to bed at 8 am when my shift ended but my body would usually allow me to sleep great for around 4 hours. A nap was usually requested a couple of hours later but by the time my next shift at the hotel rolled around, I was ready. Sometimes, when I worked on Saturday nights, we would head to church right away on Sunday morning before I slept.

I should have known that going to church or anywhere people gather after working a night shift without any sleep is extremely risky. I tend to laugh uncontrollably when my brain is tired and I am never quite sure what will trigger the laughter. If it's something a person wouldn't typically laugh at, my laughter is quiet and easily disguised. If it's something you would laugh at even when you're well rested, it would make the "up all night" me fall on the floor and roll around gasping for breath.

Due to the fact that we were Catholic, we often times attended Mass at churches other than the one we were members of and on this particular morning we found out the services alternated between the church we drove to and another one several miles away. It just so happened the services for that Sunday were at the church farther away. I was so tired and I just wanted to go home and get some sleep but instead we headed down the road and entered the church located in the neighboring town. We chose to sit on the outside end of a pew located near the back of the church. Not long after we were situated a blonde woman walked in and sat down. She positioned herself in the pew in front of us but chose to sit a bit closer to the inside aisle. Not long after she

149

was seated, the services began and everything seemed to be rolling along quite well. About three fourths into the Mass, before Communion, there was time set aside for silent prayer and it was then, when I finished my prayers and opened my eyes I caught site of the woman ahead of us. I saw her lean over just a bit to the right and all of a sudden I heard one of the healthiest doses of flatulence you could ever imagine!!!! This was the day I knew God definitely had a sense of humor and without His amazing grace, I would have ceased to exist.

I had limited options at this point. I could burst into laughter that would require my other half to carry a permit to bring a hyena to church, I could walk out, I could do my best to hold it in and fear I might release something similar or much worse or hope for lightening to shoot through the window and strike me dead! I opted to hold it in and my walk up to receive Communion was one I'll never forget. I had a smile plastered on my face that most likely scared small children and had the priest hoping I would enter his confessional immediately following the service.

When Mass had ended and we were told to go in peace to love and serve the Lord, the woman that had nearly caused my brain to explode earlier leaned over and once again released a resounding blast of thunder that shook the rafters . By this time I knew my self-control had been stretched to the limit and when I burst out the doors of that church the laughter I had held in spewed out of me like lava from a volcano!

I would never choose to disrespect anyone, especially at church, but I do believe this day helped me to realize, prayers do get answered. Some are answered in time, some are answered in ways we never imagined and some are answered within seconds of being heard!

The Shining Stars

Tonight, while at work, I felt the need to jot down some thoughts on a yellow post-it note and then, because I had no pockets, I tucked it in my bra. I went about my evening doing all the things I normally do when I close the store and the only thing that made tonight different was the tiny little scratching sensation I would get from my tiny little note that wanted to be sure I wasn't going to forget about the thoughts I had written on it earlier in the evening. Are you curious as to what I wrote? I promise I will tell you but first I want to tell you about a few of the wonderful customers that inspired me.

I was coming up one of the craft aisles when I saw a young man go whizzing past. It wasn't a typical customer spotting. This guy was wearing a rather large black helmet and he appeared to know where what he needed was. Not once did he ask me for help and when he ended up at the cutting counter beside a young girl, I decided he must have brought her to the store on his motorcycle and didn't want to risk having his helmet stolen so he wore it inside. After the fabric was cut for the young girl she walked away and he remained. It was then I realized he wasn't with the young girl and that he too had a bolt of fabric in his hands. Not wanting to make eye contact he sheepishly said, "I've never been here before and I have no idea how to do this but I would like just a small amount of this fabric." We discussed amounts and he decided on an eighth of a yard. Once it was cut he thanked me for being so helpful and nice to him and then politely asked where he should go to pay for his fabric. It was clear he had issues and difficulties dealing with things we often times take for granted but his eyes gave way to the beautiful person that was hiding inside that helmet.

Not long after he left I ran across an elderly couple and their son. It was clear their son had Down's Syndrome and it was also clear they feared how people might react to their precious son and appeared to be quite guarded. I turned down the aisle they were standing in and said, "Hi! How are you doing today?" They responded pleasantly but were very reserved. I was in search of a particular fabric for another customer so I had to ask their son if I could sneak around him and he couldn't bow out of my way fast enough. What a mannerly and incredibly kind person he was and what a reflection that was on his wonderful parents.

These two experiences are what inspired my note and finally....here is what I wrote. Some of the most pleasant of God's children face some pretty unimaginable odds.

I got to thinking about all the people I deal with on a daily basis and how unique and special they really all are. The shining stars, though, are the ones like the ones I dealt with today. Not once have I been insulted, judged or been made to feel anything but loved by those special souls. They're the ones God chooses for the heaviest of His crosses and the beauty and magic of their inner strength is one of the most amazing things we will ever witness, that is, if we view them with our hearts!

Today wasn't just good....it was extraordinary!

What Are The Chances?

I'm not exactly sure just how acquaintances become friends but I do know how they don't become friends and as fate would have it, I ran into two of those people that didn't make my friend list this past Saturday and each situation had me a bit baffled, asking myself, "What are the chances?"

I like to think I'm pretty easy to talk to and it's not often I run into people I can't communicate with. From past experience, actions and comments stemming from an all-around negative attitude are deal breakers for me and if they exist, I'm probably not going to waste a whole lot of my time around you. It's best for both of us as my powers of biting my lip are somewhat limited when I am faced with someone that finds absolutely no joy in "playing nice with others!" The two people I happened upon Saturday were actually women I used to work with. One of them was the girl that trained me to do the custom framing at a previous job nearly 30 years ago and the other was a co-worker from my present job that finally decided to move on and find a job that offered more hours and not once have I heard anyone say how sad they are that she left or how much they miss her, including me.

I actually happened upon the one that left the place where I am currently employed first and I was rather surprised at how pleasantly she reacted to me when I walked in the door of the convenience store where she is now working. I was dumbfounded to see her and even though I wasn't able to muster up the same pleasant reaction, I was civil and courteous. There were roughly 200 miles separating the two women I would encounter that day so I had time to ponder the first reunion before being confronted with yet another.

I thought about the months I worked with that woman and the negative aura that surrounded her every day. We never had any terribly heated discussions but when people lash out at me for no particular reason I tend to remove myself from situations that will involve a lot of conversing. It's my way of saying there is no place in my world for you right now. That may seem harsh but it's how I protect myself from unnecessary attacks. Once someone has established this type of standing with me I go into "observe" mode. I listen to their conversations with others. I watch how they do things and I slowly let them back in if I feel there is any hope of understanding just what has made them so incredibly bitter. There is one thing I remember her saying not long before she moved on to the job she now has and here it is: "I have no life." Four words that spoke volumes when added to all the things I had learned about her over time. At that very moment I felt compassion for someone I could barely tolerate and according to the reaction she had for me on Saturday, perhaps she knew there was actually someone in this world that understood her pain.

My next experience arrived at the checkout while at Walmart. Don was busy unloading the cart when I caught sight of the woman sliding our items past the scanner. She looked familiar but I had to get a peek at her name tag as reassurance she was who I thought she was and she was. Time had changed her appearance considerably but her eyes appeared to be the same cold, uncaring eyes they were back when they were looking down at me making me feel as small and insignificant as they possibly could. I like to believe I'm a very forgiving type person but I've also learned over time that forgiving isn't about forgetting but rather choosing to take something positive away from negative experiences. I don't hate this woman or anyone else for that matter. As time has gone on I've realized some of the most negative people are some of the most insecure people that have been angered and hurt by others one too many times. I could tell "Kris" was hoping I wouldn't remember her as she is probably three times the size she was 30 years ago and her beautifully styled blonde hair and flawless makeup have been replaced by a more realistic and approachable look but I did remember her and I told her I did. She remembered me too and mustered up a bit of guarded conversation before it was time for us to go. You could see a bit of relief in her eyes as she said goodbye and I turned around and said, "It was nice to see you. You're just as beautiful today as you always were." I didn't have to say that but I did. I didn't have to forgive her for making me feel terrible all those years ago but I did. I didn't even have to tell her I recognized her as I could tell she was hoping I wouldn't but I did. As a result of my comment, I was able to erase a pair of cold and uncaring eyes from my memory and replace them with a pair of eyes that became a window that allowed me to see beauty from within rather than beauty that covered a very cold and uncaring heart.

If it weren't for pain, would our good times feel just as good? Would we appreciate all the blessings in our lives if we were never challenged or put in situations that left us feeling unappreciated? I believe balance is the most important factor in our existence. We need some pain for growth. We need to be humbled to develop compassion. What's unfortunate is when the balance doesn't exist. In my experience with the two women I've written about, I believe they've both suffered more pain that unfortunately created a rather large void where joy should exist. I didn't enjoy knowing them because of how they treated me but not once did I believe in my heart that I had any reason to hate them. I did, however, have all the reasons in the world to say a prayer for them. Prayer is powerful and fully capable of replacing the pain in anyone's heart with joy and a balance each and every one of us needs to survive in this crazy thing called life!

The Person I've Become

I have never attended church on a regular basis. I have sort have gone in streaks over the years and I suppose it's partly due to the fact that going to church every Sunday wasn't a part of my family's routine when I was growing up. I sometimes struggle a bit with setting aside that hour once a week when I may or may not be reached by the sermon. I would be lying if I said my mind hasn't wandered when it shouldn't and I don't believe attendance is what's most important. I believe living the Word is what's important. This isn't the way a person should probably think but it's honest and it's how I feel. I believe in God. I believe in being kind, compassionate and trustworthy and I believe God's presence in my life has shaped the person I've become.

I don't remember a lot about the lessons covered before I was confirmed as a Methodist and I don't remember everything I learned when I made a decision to become Catholic but I do have some rather fond memories of a particular priest in a neighboring town that delivered two sermons that will live forever in my heart. Once you read what I recall, I think you'll understand their impact on my life as well as on your own.

Fr. Evans welcomed us into his church every time we visited, with open arms. He had a way of making people feel so special and I just happened to be one of those lucky people. The first sermon I distinctly remember was the one when he shared a story about a man that felt the cross he was bearing was simply more than he could handle. Jesus met up with the man, sensing his pain and said, "Follow Me. Let's see what we can do." The man was led into a large room filled with crosses that appeared to reach far into the sky. It was a rather unusual building, no doubt, and it did almost seem as if it had no ceiling. He was amazed by all the choices he had and he was quite happy that Jesus sensed his pain and that Jesus was willing to let him trade his large cross for one he felt he could better manage. They spent quite a bit of time looking over the inventory and eventually they came across one that looked perfect. The man told Jesus, "I think I've found the cross I want." It was then Jesus replied, "That's the one you had with you when you arrived."

It's pretty easy to convince ourselves that everyone else has life so much easier than we do. I have times when I love to feel sorry for myself. I get frustrated, anxious and just plain sad at times but God is always there for me. I struggled with thoughts as to whether He could forgive me for divorcing but I feel in my heart that He has. I still ask Him from time to time if it's okay to be happy and He always sends a rather warm feeling directly to my heart which tells me He is very okay with that idea.

The second sermon that moved me in a very big way was the morning Fr. Evans brought a small wood door to church with him. He began his sermon about baggage and how unnecessary it is. It was then he leaned over and took hold of two rather large bags. With the bags in his outstretched arms he stood behind the door in an effort to show us just how much of him wasn't going to fit through the opening that door was going to offer. He used those visuals to help us understand just how important forgiveness and letting go of all the baggage we carry with us really is. I am pretty sure you can think of someone you would have a hard time saying something nice about. We all have experiences in life that hurt us and damage a part of our heart that is not easily mended but I honestly believe there's a rather substantial amount of peace waiting on the other side of that door labeled "Forgiveness." It might not be a small wooden one like the one that always comes to mind when I think about forgiveness and baggage but we all have one that is waiting patiently for us when our time comes to finally open it.

Top Ten Driver Types

Up until a few years ago I hadn't lived in a city with stop lights. I was from Small Town America and I had no idea how much I was going to learn when stop lights became a regular part of my world. I've been taking mental notes on my commute to work and I've decided there are quite a few different types of drivers. "Down the road" I may even add a few more.

1. "The Spaz" types sit at stop lights and let up on their brakes every 3 seconds and inch ahead approximately three fourths of an inch each time until the light finally turns green. Spaz types are well known for their addictions to caffeine and sugar.

2. "The Dreamer" types use their time at stop lights to meditate and enjoy the scenery. Some have even been known to drift off. This type almost always ends up as the first car in a string of many in that same lane and studies have shown that they hear more horns than any other people on the face of the earth....coming from behind, of course.

3. "The Butt" types are the insurance risks that love to smoke and drive. One of their favorite activities is tossing their lit cigarette out the window of their moving vehicle. Isn't that littering? It's not something that just disintegrates the second it hits the ground and it's also on fire! That should mean it's okay for me to light my trash on fire and toss it

out my car window while I'm on my way to work. To heck with dumpsters. Who needs 'em?

4. "The Music Man" types drive the cars with the really dark, atomic bomb strength, tempered glass windows. They've been driving with the volume of their sound system so loud for so long that they can no longer hear it but they can feel it and it feels good. It's been determined their sound systems have been the number one reason cars without mechanical problems end up at service stations for tune ups. You've heard that low pitched thumping before. You just didn't know it wasn't coming from your car.....until now!

5. "The Blabbermouth" types are the drivers that wants to tell you a little bit about themselves. They can easily be identified by the clever little saying spelled out on their license plates, the outdoor grade vinyl stickers affixed to their back window telling you there's a dad, a mom, a boy, a girl, two dogs and one cat or a boy urinating on something. I've learned over time these drivers are among some of the happiest ones out there. They rarely cut in front of you, they don't honk at you if you do something wrong and I'm betting they're just darn nice people, even the ones that pee on stuff....harmless....I'm telling ya....good people.

6. "The Sundae Driver" types are the drivers that always end up ahead of you when you're in a hurry. I purposely spelled it the way I did as they appear to be some of the sweetest people in existence. If we weren't in so much of a hurry when we see them it would be fun to just pull into

the nearest ice cream stand and visit with them for a few minutes.

7. "The Blinkless Wonder" types are the drivers that never use turn signals. This type is better known for their ability to raise blood pressures more than stress, obesity and excessive use of salt combined. I've also heard they are the reason 4 letter words were invented. These drivers don't typically spend a lot of time making plans. They just go with the flow....that is, until it rear-ends 'em.

8. "The Device-ists" are the ones that just can't take a break from their phone for a single second. They feel an undeniable urge to call someone, text someone or surf the internet while driving because they know nothing bad really happens when you take your eyes of the road and they also know all the pictures of smashed vehicles on the internet are staged. Those things don't really happen. This type of driver is the one you will most often see zipping through red lights. They can also be found at the end of a string of cars turning well after the turn signal turns RED! They not only love their phones. They love gaming and Marvel Comics and these risks takers feel as if they're actually living out the actions of one of their favorite superheroes!

9. "The Tire Buyers" are the ones that leave their mark anywhere and everywhere they possibly can. Sometimes it's a straight line and sometimes it's curved but you won't know for sure until the smoke clears. These types of drivers may appear to be a tad bit reckless but in reality, they're some of the best drivers out there and if you ever need to travel down an icy, muddy or snow packed road,

they're going to be the ones that will keep that vehicle on the road when everyone else is sitting in the ditch.

10. And last but not least there's "The Yellow Flagger" type. This cautious driver does their best to stop when they should stop and go when they should go. They use their turn signals. They wear their seat belt and their goal is always to get from point A to point B with as little conflict as possible. They're cautious and careful most of the time. They're the type that will rescue kittens and move them to places where they'll be taken care of. Their accident history is typically short but can sometimes include collisions with well-built iron structures like windmills.

I included a few very subtle clues as to which types Don and I are just for fun. Any ideas? And also, which one are you?

The Harley In The Hall

If ever there was any doubt that opposites attract, Don and I are here to say, doubt not, opposites are indeed, attracted to one another. He is the Morning Glory in the garden of life and I, on the other hand, am the magnificent Moon Flower blooming long after the warmth of the fiery orb has left us until another day. With this delightful explanation of our somewhat different view on when one's ambition should be expended I shall move on to the story that transpired one evening when Don succumbed to the bed that was calling his name. It was 8:40pm.

After several heartfelt exchanges between our lips (kisses or smootches as we prefer to call them) I slipped into the haven (sewing room) that quietly awaits my return the very same time each and every evening. Sometimes I alter clothing, create craft videos, surf the internet or type blog posts but on this particular evening I was making dolls. When I do this I need more light, so in an effort to keep things as dark as possible for the Morning Glory, I opened the linen closet door that, when open, goes across our bedroom door opening and blocks the light that sneaks out the top of my sewing room door. I could shut the bedroom door but this just works better. Around midnight I decided to shut off the lights and head to bed. I'm sure you've been in a position to be as quiet as possible so as not to wake someone and it usually works....usually.

When I left the sewing room I saw the linen closet door and I told myself, "Oh, I'll remember this is open when I come back down the hall to get into bed. I went into the kitchen and realized the apple pie I had made earlier needed to be covered so I grabbed the tinfoil box. Do you have any idea how much noise tinfoil makes? Unbelievable! I think I counted 97 teeth along the edge of the box there to help sever the piece you are needing from the rest of the roll. Finally I managed to get what I needed separated from the box, one tooth at a time and then I pondered for a while as to how I was going to get it wrapped around the pie. The "ripping off a band-aid" mentality hit me and I whipped the foil on the pie and sealed the edges really fast and then I listened......nothing.....nothing.....snoring. Whew! He was still asleep.

Next it was time to brush my teeth. I'm happy to say this went pretty well. It was the usual noises with no surprises and Don's sub-conscience is used to that. I left the bathroom and headed down the very dark hall prepared to do what I always do. I walk into our bedroom and get into bed.

On this particular night my typical routine was somewhat altered because on this particular night, as I confidently marched towards the spot in the bedroom I always go, there was a door in my way that I had forgotten about! Do you have any idea how much noise is created by a forgetful woman running into a door as if it wasn't there? Just ask Morning Glory! He woke up.....rather abruptly as a matter of fact and told me, once his initial shock had dissipated, that the amount of noise presented by the disturbance was comparable to starting a Harley Davidson in the hall! I'm not sure why my short term memory is so pathetic and I'm not sure why I wasn't able to lessen the noise factor once I realized what was happening but there is one thing I know for sure......I hadn't had a good laugh like that for a very long time and every time I replayed Don's response in my head I laughed even harder. Eventually we both fell asleep but not until I had fully extinguished a full 12 minutes of uncontrollable, bed shaking laughter!!

Sore Puzzlers

Have you ever wondered why so many things have changed over the years and not always for the better?

I remember a time when it didn't matter if the Christmas cards you sent and received said Happy Holidays, Seasons Greetings or Merry Christmas as they all meant the very same thing. They meant that you wanted to send love and well wishes to all the people you care about during that special time of year when we gather together to celebrate the joyous birth of our Lord and Savior. I used to look so forward to designing our Christmas card but now, when I work on choosing the template, I tend to steer clear of the ones that don't say Merry Christmas for fear I'll end up offending someone. Is that really how things should be? Is that really how Christ would want it? Do you really believe the power of His existence is dependent on what words you use to address others in the days leading up to the celebration of His birth?

I realize Christ is being forced out of places He has always been welcome but do you really believe it's stopping Him or slowing His pace in any way? It's okay if you do but I choose to believe He's unstoppable. I choose to believe His presence has been, is and will always be a part of all who believe. There may be a bunch of non-believers "getting their way" and poisoning even the most innocent of minds but their war will never be won. It will rage on however, and it will do it's best to convince us that only certain words are acceptable on our Christmas cards when in reality, all pleasant wishes are acceptable. Christ lives in your heart. Christ lives in my heart. Since the very moment of His blessed birth He became a part of each and every one of us.

Let's do each other a very special favor every holiday season. Let's try to remember to love one another. Let's try to not get caught up in all the turmoil the media loves to create and let's take a very whimsical approach to our thinking with special thanks to Dr Suess when he wrote and released "How the Grinch Stole Christmas" in May of 1957 because we all know.....

"It will come without ribbons. It will come without tags. It will come without packages, boxes or bags. We'll puzzle and puzzle 'till our puzzlers are sore. Then we'll all think of something we hadn't before. Christmas, we'll know, doesn't come from a store. Christmas, perhaps, means a little bit more."

"Texted" To The Max

Ways To Tell If The Relationship You've Established With Your Cell Phone Is Perhaps, A Bit, "Over The Top!"

You slowly begin to wake from a restful night's sleep and rather than give that first sip of coffee your full attention, you grab your phone to see if anyone messaged you, poked you or revealed some incredibly fantastic news on Facebook after you dozed off the night before that you just have to know more than anything in the world.

You learn that sitting on the toilet too long will actually cause your legs to "fall asleep." Yes, it's true. They get tired of waiting for you to check all of your messages while propped up on that hollow circle that inevitably restricts the blood flow to them and they have no other choice. Once you remove yourself, you learn rather quickly legs aren't real happy when you "wake" them up.

You begin to wonder why so many people are saying, "I told you this about a week ago, don't you remember?" and then you realize it might have something to do with the fact that you were somewhat distracted by a story about a dress that looks white with touches of gold in some pictures and blue with touches of black in others. Hmmm, this is interesting stuff, no doubt.

Your whole life is being conveniently stored on your phone. Your family's birthdays, your grocery list, your business contacts, your results from your pregnancy test provided you purchased your phone with the optional "pee stick" attachment. Your phone is no longer a means of communication between you and another person for a small amount of time but rather a device that has given you the confidence to share everything you can possibly think of just in case you forget everything about yourself and all at the very same time.

You go out to eat with friends but carry on a text conversation with someone else the entire time you could be laughing and carrying on with real people sitting within 3 feet of you.

You feel the need to call home to make sure you pick up the right kind of shampoo. We all know shampoos are all different and the reason manufacturers create 7000 different kinds is because there are 7000 different ways people can get their hair dirty.....of course.

Due to the fact that you have a very busy and productive life, you need to make use of every single second of every single day so you save your chats with yours friends for those times when you sit down in the stall of a public restroom. It's so darn handy to have that phone with you and I'd be willing to bet your friend can't even tell where you are if you pretend to sneeze or cough during the "splash down" and flush parts of your mission.

Your friends wouldn't describe you as the "chatterbox" type but for some reason, you can always think of someone to call while you're at the store and you've learned the best time to get into a really involved chat is when it's time to check out. The people ringing up your sale don't mind. They love trying to slip in a few pertinent questions when they notice you taking a breath. (Okay, I'm kidding. They're really entertaining thoughts of slapping you up in an attempt to get your attention for the better part of 3 minutes.)

You may or may not be aware of this yet but when you are out in public talking on your phone, YOU ARE TALKING A LOT LOUDER THAN YOU THINK YOU ARE.

You are into fitness and you take regular walks. You've been attached to your phone so long that you are now able to walk without watching where you're going and you almost never run into anything except an occasional stop sign, that guy on the skateboard, the woman with the stroller, the trash can, the garage sale sign, the guy wearing the furniture store sign advertising a big sale and the parked car but those things happen to everyone....the phone DID NOT distract you.

This story was inspired by a letter to "Dear Abby" I read earlier about a parent that was so let down by her adult children when they arrived at her house for a birthday party. No one offered to help clear the table, do the dishes or watch the children but rather sat around each staring at their cell phones or tablets while she did all the work. It's just another story of a very good and helpful invention gone terribly wrong in some instances. It's nothing new, this type of thing happens all the time.

(No, cell phones don't come with a "pee stick" attachment......not yet anyway but I like the fact that I had you wondering! Sorry. It makes reading my work more fun as you never know what I'll say next.)

Do You Glow?

We have a large bin filled with neon play balls near our checkouts and today when things got busy, I headed up front to help out. Those balls grasp the attention of almost all the kids that walk through the door and today there were 3 young boys that decided to play a round of basketball with them. Balls were flying in every direction. I let it go on until I finished with my customer and then I asked them to stop and pick up all the balls that had landed on the floor. I explained my concern that someone may trip on them and fall down. The boys listened very well and within seconds the balls were all back in the bin. By then we had gotten caught up with people in line so I decided to visit with the boys while their mothers finished checking out. I saw that one of them had a can of glow in the dark slime so I asked if I could see it. He said, "This was a rip off. It doesn't even glow." The littlest one of the three piped up and said, "Sure it will. You just have to feed it some light!" I agreed and told him he might just be surprised by his blob of slime tonight, when he shuts the lights off if he did get a chance to "feed" it some light.

Before long I had all three boys gathered near me and they were quite the pleasant little visitors. They said they found all kinds of things in the ball bin that didn't belong in there including a fidget and it wasn't until then that I noticed the littlest boy had only one finger on each of his hands. It didn't seem to bother him in the least as he tried to carefully balance that fidget on one finger and spin it with the other.

It's moments like this that put life back into perspective. It's so easy to forget how blessed we are with 10 fingers that all work, 2 legs that carry us around, 2 ears that hear and 2 eyes that see. It's also easy to forget our positive attitude at home and blame the entire world for our problems but this fine young man is making the most of what he has. His 2 legs allowed him to run all over, his 2 hands allowed him to toss balls into the air, his 2 ears allowed him to hear me when I asked him to help pick up the balls on the floor and his two bright eyes clearly displayed his positive attitude. He was an inspiration for anyone willing to allow him to be and not for one second did he feel sorry for himself. He bounced and tossed balls, he made a fidget spin and he even knew that in order to get glow in the dark slime to glow, you must first feed it some light!

It seems that every once in a while life tosses in a lesson on perspective. You might never see it coming but it sure has a way of making a lasting impression. I guess you could say it's the light that makes us "glow" in those dark times when we lose sight of our countless blessings.

Sand In My Hourglass

It's not uncommon to find myself in conversations about how much fun it is to accomplish something using scraps from a left over project or better yet, creating something that cost nothing. It's pretty safe to say thoughts like that are formed from a childhood that involved a wealth of imagination due to the fact that there was nothing else available. These thoughts often times lead us into a bit of reminiscing about our younger days and it's not uncommon to discuss all the mud pies, breads and cookies we created as a part of our regular routine.

I remember our "sand" box. It was a big old tractor tire filled with mostly gravel, a bit of dirt and sand if you were willing to dig deep enough. We knew the sand was in short supply so we learned not to waste it. The one thing I distinctly remember using it for were the loaves of banana bread I prepared. The sand became the cinnamon and sugar I would sprinkle ever so lightly on those loaves before they were set in the sun to "bake."

Some of the other things discussed are the ways we would spend our summer vacation. I remember walking a lot and I also remember putting a ton of miles on my bike. Learning to drive before I hit double digits just didn't happen and even after I did learn to drive, the car wasn't something I was going to be using for short trips around town when I had two feet and a bike. I remember spending time with my friends from sun up to sun down. I remember swinging on the swings, bouncing up and down on the teeter totter, sliding down the slide, slipping a loop around my ankle that had a string attached and a bell at the other end and I remember swinging that bell and hopping over it several hundred times before summer vacation came to a close. I remember playing with my barbies and baby dolls and drawing numbers on the sidewalk so that my friends and I could attempt to hop on one foot all the way to 10! I remember sitting on the tire hump in the back of the old pickup hanging onto the five gallon buckets while we bounced down the road searching for plums and chokecherries. I remember playing "Don't Break The Ice," "Don't Spill The Beans" and "Ants In The Pants" too but those were saved for rainy days. We ate Popsicles and Mr. Freezes and watched in total disbelief when the swirled tin foil cover on the Jiffy Pop popcorn began to rise right before our very eyes!

I'm sure the kids today will have a comparable amount of fond memories from their childhoods. They'll most likely be considerably different than what I remember from mine and that's okay. I just hope the magnetic charm of technology doesn't completely replace the honest to goodness feel you can only get from actually doing something rather than watching someone else do it "online."

There really is nothing like the smell of a bucket of plums sitting in the back porch waiting to become jelly or the feel of dirt packed tightly under each fingernail after a hard day at the "bakery" and there's nothing more worth hanging onto than a time in your life when everything about it was sweet and innocent and filled with heaping helpings of unimaginable joy!

Missing Yellow Ribbons

For years the neighbors planted a garden on the very back corner of their lot that butted up to the very edge of our yard. Perhaps I'm wrong, but every year it seemed like the tilled ground of their garden began to creep further and further onto our property. People coming to visit would often times compliment my nice looking garden and were somewhat surprised when I would tell them it wasn't mine. Nothing was ever mentioned but it sort of bugged me. After about 14 years and 14 inches of lost ground later I decided to hire someone to come over and till up a spot for me so I could plant a garden. I thought it might be sort of fun to have some fresh produce and I sort of figured it might be the only way to stop the neighbor from adding the "inch a year" to his garden spot.

I mapped out my plan and was told by the guy I hired to do the tilling that I would "clearly" mark the corners of where he should till so that just in case I wasn't home when he got there, he would know exactly where to go. A few windy days later he showed up at the post office where I worked and told me he got the tilling done so I paid him and anxiously awaited closing time so I could go home and hit the dirt!

As I strolled into the driveway after work I expected to see a small patch of black dirt to be visible from where I parked but everything looked just exactly as it did when I had left for work. Hmmm....I wondered what had happened. The tiller guy had worked for me before and there was never a problem but the ground that was marked was clearly untouched. I didn't see my yellow ribbons but the wind had been sort of crazy so I wondered if maybe they had gotten blown away.

I knew there had to be a logical explanation. Here are the results of my investigation.

When choosing who should till your garden, I've learned the town drunk isn't the best choice. Now don't get me wrong, he was a very nice man and he did a lot of odd jobs for people to make a little spending money so he could hop on his lawn mower and head to the bar for a few after a long hard day of tilling gardens and spraying weeds. I'm sure you're wondering why I added the part about him hopping on his lawn mower to head to the bar but that was his main vehicle after losing his driver's license for the gazillionth time due to the fact that he was driving under the influence more than he was not driving under the influence.

When I finally found him to ask him where my tilled garden spot was he looked at me in total and complete disbelief. He was shocked that I would ask him that but as the conversation went on, his shock would end up being almost undetectable in comparison to the one that I was about to experience!

Apparently the wind had indeed removed my yellow ribbons that were marking my garden spot by the time he and his tiller had gotten to my back yard. He took a look around and the only markers he could see were in ground that already appeared to be tilled but he thought to himself, this is their yard and there are sticks in the ground so this must be where I'm supposed to till.

The garden spot he discovered was our neighbor's. He was right, it had already been tilled. The sticks he saw were marking the rows of the seeds that had already been planted and all I could do was laugh....uncontrollably....almost crazy like....for a few minutes longer than I probably should have.

It just goes to show that we should all strive to do what's right. We shouldn't be greedy with anything, especially with the size of our garden if it means we have to inch our way onto our neighbor's property. Karma always finds a way to teach us lessons and sometimes it comes disguised as a tipsy guy with a tiller!

Don's "Rare" Find

I just finished reading a story on Facebook about four women that chose to attend a meeting in outfits that left very little to the imagination. There was a lot of cleavage and more bare skin than there probably needed to be and the chairman chose to address these women and the choices they made while rummaging through their closets before they arrived. He explained that everything God made valuable in this world is well covered and hard to find. He made comparisons between diamonds, gold and pearls and incorporated the similarities between them as far as how they're discovered. I'm not sure about you but I've never run across a diamond in my rock collection or a gold nugget while wading around in a pond nor have I ever seen pearls rolling around in the sand on a beach. They're well-hidden which makes them precious, valuable and highly desired.

The chairman went on to tell the women that they were far more precious than any of the things he had mentioned prior and that in order to find "miners" worthy of them, they should really rethink the choices they make when they are preparing themselves for the day ahead.

I was immediately able to identify with what this chairman had to say due to the fact that my sister, my brother and I were raised in very conservative surroundings. Showing some skin hasn't been an easy thing for any of us to do. My sister is in her mid 50's and has just now started wearing tank tops. I've never seen my brother in a pair of shorts and you won't see me prancing around in anything that might give anyone a reason to think I'm even the least bit uninhibited. When I read that story on Facebook it solidified the ideology instilled in me at a very young age and it helped me to realize it's probably more okay to be as reserved and modest as I am than it is to be a bit too comfortable in my own skin!

Don is way more comfortable in the skin he's in and he sometimes has a hard time understanding his "rare" find. As time goes on, he may be able to "unearth" small amounts of the treasures he feels I possess but deep down inside, I think he's quite happy with his discovery, no matter how thick her shell appears to be!

Andrea's Precious Soul

I wasn't able to birth babies but the bond I share with three of my nieces is one of the most amazing experiences I've ever enjoyed and I believe that what we have is the next best thing to actually bringing them into this world. I've decided to share a story about each one and the impact they have had on my life.

I'm starting with the one born first and the one that refused to arrive while I was staying with her parents, to act as moral support and errand girl while they stumbled and fumbled around as first time parents. I suppose I could have taken this as a sign that she wasn't going to like me but in reality I think she could sense the tension and excitement of three people waiting for her arrival and she decided two was going to be enough so I traveled back home and waited for "the call."

Now every year when July 26th rolls around we're reminded of the day Andrea arrived and as times goes on we continue to witness God's purpose for her and all the beautiful ways she touches not only our lives but many others along the way. I could say she's perfect and always sweet and never bossy and stubborn but that wouldn't be true and that wouldn't describe the person I know and love. She's human and she has moments, like all of us, when she's almost impossible to understand. She does, however, have other times when the depth of her kind and loving heart is, in my opinion, immeasurable. Her arrival turned me into "Aunt B" and it's a role I've cherished and will continue to cherish as time goes on.

We're all adults now and when the time came to tell my nieces I was divorcing their uncle I waited and told Andrea last as I feared she would take it the worst. It's comparable to a death due to the fact that it changes the family structure. I will never forget her reaction. It says so much about the depth of her loving heart.

We were all asked to join Andrea and her husband Shawn at a restaurant to celebrate their wedding anniversary and her birthday. I hadn't told her about the divorce yet and feared someone might say something about it during supper so I knew I had to call her that afternoon. I felt bad that I had waited so long and hoped this news wouldn't ruin this joyful day for her. Later as we began to gather for the celebration I locked eyes with Andrea and she said, "Aunt B, I have something for you. Can we go to the restroom together?"

We excused ourselves from everyone and once we reached the restroom she handed me a card and a gift. This was yet another time I called upon the grace of God to keep me upright and composed as I witnessed one of the most selfless and kindest acts another person has ever bestowed upon me. The gift was a book about the true inner strength of a woman and the card read:

To Aunt B,

Let Go and Let God

Words of Hope and Encouragement

When you're searching for truth and you can't find your way, when people don't hear what you're trying to say, and the answers won't come to the things that you pray--it's time to let go and let God. Let go of the bad and the good will appear. Trust in the knowledge that He's always near, that answers and choices are always more clear when you let go and let God. Just lift up your hands and surrender your heart, tell Him your worries and He'll do His part. Let go of the past and your future will start, when you finally let go and let God. May prayers and faith and knowing you're loved carry you through times of doubt and lead you to perfect peace.

This came from the niece I was so afraid to share my bad life changing news with as I feared she just simply would not understand. This came from an amazingly strong woman that took the time to find ways to comfort her Aunt B when her Aunt B needed it the most. This came from someone that should have been thinking about her party and what she was going to wear but instead decided to go out and search for a tangible way to say, I love you and I'm here for you.

Andrea works as a CNA and has for years. In my opinion a CNA job is one of the toughest jobs ever created if you do it right and by the looks on all the faces of the residents she introduced me to when I agreed to a tour of where she works, she is definitely "doing it right!" She has overcome some rather difficult odds over the course of her childhood, teen years and now as an adult and I'm proud of her unwavering spirit and love for her family.

This story is very personal but sharing it gives me joy and I believe our purpose in life is to spread joy whenever and wherever we can. Andrea is unique and has her very own way of showing the world who she is. Not everyone is willing to give her a chance but for those who do, God smiles upon you.

The Retail Truth

As I raised my smoked turkey sandwich dangerously close to my mouth trap, I caught sight of one of my co-workers running into the break room and she said, in a rather exasperated tone, "I need a second before I go back out there!" I would compare her demeanor to that of a person that had just been chased by a ferocious dog. She explained that she had just helped several customers that were destined to drive her completely crazy and that a little break from the action would give her attitude adjuster time to kick in. I told her I completely understood what she was saying and then I told her about one of the people I had helped earlier. I said, "Something happened today that I have never had happen here before. My customer almost made me cry." Immediately she displayed a shocked expression and said, "None of mine were that mean." and then I said, "No, that wasn't it, let me explain."

A very pleasant woman approached the counter with one bolt of baby blue flannel that had little white clouds and little yellow moons on it. I asked her how much she was going to need and she said, "Two yards." I asked what she was going to be making with this adorable flannel and nothing could have prepared me for what she was about to say. She took a breath and this is what followed:

"My daughter is pregnant with twins and only one of them is going to live. This fabric is going to be a blanket for the one that isn't going to survive. His brain didn't develop so his head is filled with cysts. In order to save his twin, my daughter has to carry him until his twin is ready to be born so in the meantime she is planning his funeral and asked if I could make a blue blanket for him that has clouds on it. I think this fabric will work out very well, don't you?" After swallowing the rather large lump that had formed in my throat I agreed and then said how sorry I was that her daughter had to be going through such a painful and life changing experience. We visited a bit longer and shared similar experiences of the miscarriages we went through in our younger days. We also both agreed that God has a reason for everything that happens and that it sometimes takes years to completely understand just what that reason is. Eventually she offered a pleasant smile, thanked me for helping her and walked away. I, on the other hand, slipped a bolt of baby blue flannel into the "items to be put away" cart knowing I would never look at those tiny little white clouds the same, ever again.

I might make it sound like working with people in a retail sense is one of the worst jobs a person can have but in reality I know the tough ones make me stronger, the funny ones make me laugh, the grouchy ones force me to brush up on my "kill 'em with kindness" techniques and the ones with heavy hearts give me a chance to deliver a bit of compassion where it's needed most.

Gray, Gray Go Away

Back when I was in my early 20's I would venture to say I tried at least 5 different hair colors. I got pretty good at the process but the day I chose to perfect "Auburn" is the day I said goodbye to hair color for 26 years. It's a rather sad story as it took place in the early 1980's before "kool-aid" colors for hair were publicly accepted. I thought I chose well when I chose a nice rich shade of auburn and I really thought I had it right so as soon as my freshly altered locks were dry and curled, the desire to flaunt this fiery new shade led me right into the only store there was in the tiny little town that I lived. I was super confident with my new look when I sailed in the door. That is until I received my first review and that incredibly audible voice said, "Hey Bev, I like your hair! It matches your sweatshirt!" I wish I could tell you I was wearing a deep rust colored sweatshirt but in reality, the sweatshirt was pink. The wind that had originally filled my sails stopped abruptly and once my sails.......err, ah, I mean feet hit the ground, they were running!

Tonight, after 26 years, I decided to give hair color another chance but the reason varied slightly from the 1980's "I'm bored and hair color is cheap" mentality I had used before. This time I selected a light ash brown that may perhaps lessen the appearance of the gray highlights that have been making their presence known for several years now. I expected the process to be as simple as it was 26 years ago but I read the instructions anyway and decided, just like then, not to do the allergy test first. I was ready to do this now and not 48 hours from now so I tossed the possibility of losing every strand of hair on my head to the wind and soon the "fun" began.

Due to the fact that I love to live on the edge at times and exhibit a bit too much confidence when it comes to not spilling things I opted to wear the white tank top I had on under my gray sweater. I own a light ash brown top but I didn't wear it. Here's bit of advice for you. If you decide to color your own hair, wear a shirt that closely matches the project taking place on the top of your head. I didn't....I should have. I also decided to use the shower head on the hose thing to rinse out the dye rather than the kitchen sink when my 25 minutes had passed and that ended up being my second mistake.

I learned that they are right when they tell you the dye will sting if it gets in your eyes and that when letting go of the shower head on the hose thing while the water is running causes it to spin around in circles and I learned that laying the towel for your head on the edge of the tub when you're wrestling a shower head on a hose thing is a bad idea if you want it to stay dry. I learned that I could get completely undressed with one hand while the other was on the spinning shower head and that it is entirely possible to take a tank top off without taking it over your light ash brown, dye drenched head!

I'm all showered now and ready for bed. My hair looks great and tomorrow, when I get the courage to enter the bathroom again I hope the light ash brown dye looks as good on the shower walls, the shower curtains, the floor, the towels, the rugs and the white tank top as it does on my silky smooth, luxurious hair! It's sort of a shame that no one will be here to tell me, "Hey Bev, I like your hair! It matches your shower walls, shower curtains, the bathroom floor, the towels, the rugs and the spots on your white tank top!"

Womanhood - A Graphic Version

Often times I find myself entering into conversations that are fueled by a continuous string of thoughts and after the fact, as I relive the highlights, I find myself wondering if the subject originally presented had anything to do with the direction things headed when all those thoughts and memories came running up to the podium fighting for their chance to be heard.

Tonight, at work, a much younger co-worker and I ended up in a rather whimsical conversation about the joys of being a woman. Due to the fact that I'm almost twice her age, I had a pretty substantial pile of musty stories that were looking pretty impressive once they were dusted off. I planned to present them as tactfully as I could but I decided to let her go first. I was confident with what I had to work with and I was pretty sure that whatever she was about to tell me could not even begin to compare to the levels of embarrassment I have been forced to digest in my 49 years. Keep in mind, this conversation lasted less than 2 minutes and it happened when there were no customers present....we have scruples.....we do.

She said, "I will never forget the day I had my stent removed after my kidney stone episode. It was so embarrassing. The doctor had a camera and a probe inside my bladder and I could see my bladder on a TV screen so I attempted to make casual conversation about how that was something you don't see every day." At this point I had found the perfect opportunity to take center stage. I asked her if she had ever had a sterile urine sample taken. She hadn't and is now quite certain she never wants to. The nurse that got this lovely job when my legs and thighs were a mile high in the sky most likely did a little rethinking when it came to her career choice. She took a tiny little tube and made at least 12 attempts to poke it into my bladder opening and according to my experience, I have a very small bladder opening and it's apparently, very difficult to locate.

On another occasion during that "time of the month" I found myself feeling around for that tiny little string that is always, always.......always attached to your feminine protection and for some reason, it wasn't there. Hmmm.....where could it have gone? You don't really believe it isn't there so you check a second time........and a third time........and then a fourth time. At this point the thought process begins. What should I do? I AM NOT GOING TO THE DOCTOR! That was the only thing I was sure of at the moment. As the minutes ticked by my heart began to race and I thought of all kinds of crazy things that could happen and once my overactive brain had elevated my blood pressure to the point of blowing the top of my head clean off I found myself.....calling the clinic. I learned that for this type of office call, a sense of humor is very helpful. It happened quite a few years ago but I can still remember how closely the nurse was watching what the doctor was doing and I envisioned her with a huge bucket of popcorn and a box of Junior Mints. The movie had one of those cliff hanger type endings. Diagnosis: The doctor couldn't find the string either or anything else for that matter. After this life changing experience I removed the possibility of it ever happening again and the only down side I've noticed so far is when I get the feeling I have just given birth to a jellyfish every time I cough or sneeze during that lovely "time of the month."

I remember another time when I was in my early 20's and I saw my doctor for my annual physical which included a PAP smear. I realize doctor's see things like what he saw every day but I've always been very modest and I tend to grit my teeth the entire

182

time I am put in such a compromising position. I'm always glad when it's over and there's a whole 12 months ahead before I have to do it again. After something like that I don't want to see the doctor back in the examination room, in the hallway, at the nurse's station or anywhere else for that matter, for an entire year, if at all possible. It just weirds me out! I wish there was a different way to accomplish what needs to happen but so far, it's still feet in the air, thighs to the sky and I hate it. After my appointment I went back to work and a dear friend of mine stopped in and asked if I wanted to meet her for supper. I accepted the invite and once my work day was complete I had sort of let go of my earlier humiliation and decided to just relax and eat tacos and laugh with my friend. We got to the restaurant about the same time, placed our orders and just as we sat down to eat guess who walked in. MY DOCTOR!!!!! If I had gone in for a stuffy nose or a sore throat it wouldn't have been any big deal but running into your doctor at a restaurant just after he finished collecting microscopic bits of things I don't even want to think about was just not my idea of something that should happen....ever. Obviously I survived this horrendous humiliation but it still weirds me out just thinking about it.

I can't honestly remember what was said to spark such an embarrassing compilation of stories but whatever it was wasn't nearly as thought provoking as the stories we both remembered when we got the chance to wear paper towel clothes and listen to our hearts pound out a beat that could shatter glass while our skin produced goose bumps the size of Mt St Helen's! Ah yes, the joys of being a woman....the graphic version, indeed!

Precious Little Poop Poop

I did something today that would amaze some and leave others in total and complete disbelief. I made curtains for my sewing room with flawed fabric!!!! A while back I purchased two rather large yardages of cream colored taffeta and both of them had some snags and several spots. I could have fin-angled a way to avoid almost all of the "deal breakers" but I'm just not that fussy so I pulled one of the pieces out of the bag and measured it. As fate would have it, that piece was long enough for two panels so I finished the edges on both of them, hems were next and last but not least I finished the rod pockets on both. I saw a few spots when I was ironing them but once they were hung it was almost as if the spots completely disappeared! They're gorgeous, they're exactly what I wanted and they're done and not once did I have a melt down at the store when I saw those unimaginable flaws. I just dealt with it.

I probably shouldn't pick on the "fussy fart" types I deal with on a regular basis but they do have several very predictable reactions in common. First they overreact. "OH MY GOSH! There's a spot!!! This fabric is going to be a blanket for our precious little poop poop and that will just not do!!! No, No, NO!

Second, once they find out there is no more fabric with navy blue and aqua airplanes, the pregnant daughter tosses a pout in "first time grandma-to-be's" direction as an indication that she expects another bolt of the same fabric to magically appear due to the fact that it's WHAT SHE WANTS! I usually let them stew for a while and then offer the fabric to them at a discount. Once they hear they are going to get the navy blue and aqua airplanes at a cheaper price they are ready willing and able to accept the fact

184

that a few of the planes have a bit more "exhaust" than some of the others. Little poop poop will probably poop on it anyway and life will go on. I always chuckle when something can go from "TOTALLY UNACCEPTABLE!" to "I think we can make this work." when the price goes down!

There are times the flaws really are unacceptable, even to me and those circumstances are much easier to deal with in my mind as well as at the cutting counter. It's the tiniest of the tiny flaws that seem to draw the most attention, however. The spots on the airplane fabric were about the size of the head of a pin!

I'll bet I sound like the world of retail is finally starting to erode the protective cover that houses my sanity but it really isn't. There are days I want to smack people but over time you tend to develop coping strategies that your customers will never know anything about and it's those strategies that help me to maintain a somewhat civil presence when the "navy blue and aqua airplanes" are crashing all around me!

Entrusted

Everyone embarks on their very own individual journey. We're created, we develop and the very second we're born, our adventure begins. We begin to learn and grow from the very moment our birth is recorded and there are no two journeys exactly the same. It's really quite remarkable, when you take the time to think, just how unique we really are and how each and every circumstance we encounter shapes us and molds our mental, spiritual and physical being. I spend a lot of time, not only trying to make sense of my own destiny, but to try and understand other's as well and I find myself the most intrigued when my path crosses that of someone who appears to throw boulders into mine. I've always tried to convince myself these "boulder throwers" must have a reason for making my life more difficult but coming up with a reason why would always take center stage when the Lord and I would visit at the end of the day. I have prayed and prayed for the knowledge to understand why some people appear to enjoy the process of making me question nearly every word I say and every thought I think. One such individual, in particular, has taken up quite a bit of room in my thoughts lately and quite honestly, I don't think I have ever been more hurt by anyone in my entire life. The prayers and tears and days have come and gone and I can honestly say I wasn't sure the answer would ever arrive as nothing really appeared to be changing.

Prayer is such an interesting phenomenon. We offer our thoughts and innermost feelings to our Great and Powerful Savior and then, when nothing appears to be changing we wonder if He heard our prayer. Isn't being human sad at times? We honestly lose faith and start to believe we really aren't heard. We convince ourselves there really isn't comfort coming and we even start to believe nothing is going to change.....

And then......

Somethings changes.

I'm not sure about you but from my own experience, the answers to my prayers never arrive like a letter in the mailbox, plain and clear, black and white. I would describe the answer to a prayer to that of water being introduced to very dry soil. The water gently touches the hard, sun baked surface and is slowly absorbed. Eventually the cracks dissolve and the change is evident.

At times we hear the voice of God but from my experience it isn't nearly as theatrical as movies might suggest. For me it's like words I hear, ever so gently introduced into my thoughts that had never occurred to me before. From my most recent experience the words I heard helped me to realize I tend to view myself as a victim when in reality, that is not my intended role. From this most recent hurtful and very painful experience I have been praying about, the words I heard said,

"I didn't put this difficult person in your life......I put you in theirs."

From the moment I heard those words I realized I wasn't a victim at all but rather chosen to share some of the glorious compassion I witness from our dear Lord and Savior each and every day. I was no longer someone that could be hurt by venomous words but rather someone God entrusted to attempt to bring this soul closer to Him.

It's only been a month since this "change" has taken place and I'm sure there will still be moments when I struggle with this person but what's different now is something in me has changed and that something has helped me to realize that sometimes what we pray for will not change the situation but it will change the way we perceive it.

Our Inner "Facets"

Most natural diamonds are formed at high temperature and pressure at depths of 140 to 190 kilometers (87 to 118 mi) in the Earth's mantle. Carbon-containing minerals provide the carbon source, and the growth occurs over periods from 1 billion to 3.3 billion years (25% to 75% of the age of the Earth).

I'm not sure why, but it's the tough times in my life that tend to inspire the most thought. Thoughts that go way beyond the surface. Thoughts that force me to dig deep into every corner of my existence in an effort to better understand why pain is such an essential part of life. There isn't a soul in this world that can honestly say they love the times when life is at its absolute worst. We tend to gravitate towards the times in life that bring us joy, but if you think about it, those joyful moments would lose a lot of their luster if they weren't brought to the surface following some of our darkest hours.

I got to thinking about diamonds and how similar they are to our existence. We're born with all the necessary "elements" to live out the days the Lord has planned for us and over time we experience ups and downs, highs and lows and as the years come and go we begin to realize why everything we've faced had a purpose. We learn something valuable from every experience and it strengthens us as we move forward. There are times when the pressure seems almost unbearable and the dark moments feel as if they will never end but with each unbearable moment a new "facet" is formed on our soul. Over time many "facets" are created and although their formation was gained from incredible pain they shine brightly from within our heart. As we move forward we find ourselves in the company of others suffering with pain similar to pain we've experienced and we're given the opportunity to call upon our "facets." Can you imagine a world where no one ever said, "I know how you feel" or "I've been there and I promise, there are better days ahead." Words like this would never be spoken if there was no pain and no suffering. It's a bit ironic if you think about it......pain can actually bring comfort, hope and even joy when the experience gained from it is shared with others enduring a "facet" forming time in their life.

I never really knew how long it took for a diamond to form or just how but after a small amount of research I couldn't help but see the similarities between those incredible stones and our existence. The intense heat and pressure for over a billion years brings forth one of the strongest substances known to man. It sparkles and shines and is readily given as a token of deep love. Our pain, stress and feelings of unworthiness and our moments of despair when we are sure we simply cannot take another step change us and that change, once unearthed, sparkles and shines and when shared, is received as a token of deep love for others.

July, June & January

I've never been easy to surprise. It's almost as if, for most of my life, I've had a sixth sense about plans being made to surprise me. It may be partially due to the fact that my mother couldn't keep a secret if she knew it was going to make someone happy. Wrapped presents were her downfall. She would let us open a few presents from beneath the tree in early December, play for a while and then re-wrap them and always said, "You'll forget what's in them by the time Christmas gets here."

I remember, years ago, unwrapping a package that was under the Christmas tree, several times before Christmas. (This happened before Dad started taking Mom Christmas shopping for us on December 24th. Dad wasn't home a lot but he appeared to be incredibly perceptive, just sayin.) It was a little yellow, and I do mean yellow haired doll. She was dressed in a fabulous little red tutu and your fingers, when inserted into the legs of her tights, became her legs. She had little red rubbery ballerina slippers that fit on the tips of your fingers to complete the ensemble and once they were in place she was ready to dance.

My sister received one as well but the memory of her opening hers before the official "rip the wrapping paper off" day escapes me. She was older than me and for some reason, a little more likely to follow the rules of the game, if you know what I mean. When I think back I sort of wonder just how big of a little brat I was. I don't remember being the kind of kid that would hound my mother until she gave in to whatever I wanted but maybe I was. I suppose it doesn't really matter now. I know she loved me with every last ounce of her being and I know how much joy it gave her to see people happy, especially me!

Mom's love of seeing people happy was a trait she passed on to me so when my amazing niece got engaged July 31st of 2015, she and her fiancé began planning their big day. What I loved most about their plans is the fact that they chose to include me when it came to designing the invitations and the decorations for the wedding! I knew I could come up with something fun and exciting and due to the fact that this aunt grew up very "financially modest" I would most likely be able to save them some money! I considered this a win-win for all of us as they needed a bit of direction in the creativity department and I just happened to come with a deluxe set of creativity!

Over the course of the months leading up to this monumental event, Allison feared she would eventually overwhelm me with all the details she was entrusting me with and pondered ways she might be able to pay me for the "services rendered." I told her how silly she was and that I expected absolutely nothing more that her happiness on this special day. When I decorate, I experience an escape from all reality and if your life is anything like mine, you have moments, typically work related, that tend to stress you out. Finding an "escape" as I refer to it, is worth more than any pay I could ever receive, especially when it comes to a niece you dearly love and the handsome love of her life she plans to turn into your nephew!!!

The months passed by so quickly and on the night of the rehearsal supper something happened that I will never forget. The hours leading up to this moment in time included a very busy day filled with laughter, joyful conversations and lots and lots of decorating. The venue sparkled with touches of Ant B's creativity made possible by all the amazing helpers that arrived ready to follow whatever directions they would receive. The wedding day was just a day away and the excitement in the air could have been sliced and served as dessert but instead, real desserts, the decadent variety, were savored by almost every taste bud in attendance. Eventually the bride and groom stepped away from their table and gathered everyone's attention. Bits and pieces of what transpired seem to be a bit hazy for me but I do remember them passing out gifts to all the people they wanted to thank for their willingness to share in the magic of their special day. I also remember Allison talking about a "special" gift they planned to give and it was then they called Ant B up to stand with them. I saw a little box in Allison's hand and I remember her referring to me as her and her sisters "second mom." Just seeing this little box tied with curling ribbon made me think of my mom, knowing it was added in her memory. Allison and her sisters put so much thought into everything they do and I hope they know just how much space they occupy within their auntie's heart.

The gold wrapped box was placed into my hands and due to the fact that Allison knew how tough curling ribbon is, she also handed me a pocket knife so the struggle to reveal the contents of the box wouldn't take as long as it would have without the adequately equipped knife blade. At this moment, I had no idea what I was going to uncover once the gift wrap was removed. I was pretty sure it wasn't a set of Pyrex bowls, a pizza pan or a 24" garden hedgehog statue (hey, they got a lot of cool shower gifts I thought they might want to share with me) but what it was, I never saw coming.

Eventually the unwrapped box revealed yet another box. This one was made of black velvet which might tell an unknowing aunt that it could possibly be jewelry or saved baby teeth. All I knew is it was going to be something very special.

As I slowly opened the tiny little velvet box my heart began to pound.

I had never felt more special in my entire life. I had uncovered the mystery of that "special gift" chosen by a bride and groom that forever changed the way their Ant B would see herself.

Not only is she an aunt, but to her incredibly precious nieces, she is also a mom....a second mom with a breathtaking "Mother's" ring to prove it!

The Gas Powered Cats

Layer by layer, I slowly prepared myself for our Saturday afternoon snowmobiling adventure. First the daily undergarments were added to my frame. Once in place I scrunched up my pantyhose and slid each one of my legs into those nasty "I now know what baloney feels like" casings. A pair of socks and a pair of jeans followed and then a turtleneck top was seated directly beneath a nice warm sweatshirt. Earlier in the week I purchased a pair of snow pants complete with buckles and suspenders that were clearly designed for Paul Bunyan or the Jolly Green Giant. I quickly learned that the ridiculously long straps forming the suspenders were quite easily cinched up if you were willing to slam one end of them in the very nearby bedroom door while making a serious attempt to walk away.

Finally the time had arrived to debut my "It's -10 and I'm going to be warm" look to the love of my life. As crazy and hard as it is to believe, he just chuckled but entered no legible comments. This proves one of two things. Number one, he didn't want to go out snowmobiling alone or Number two, he valued some of the parts he would be tucking into his snow pants, if you know what I mean! It's safe to say I looked scarier than the abominable snowman on Rudolph, The Red Nosed Reindeer and I knew if I stayed away from mirrors and avoided looking at the pictures Don snapped with his phone everything would be just fine.

We drove to my brother's repair shop to install the rest of our gear which included coats, boots, gloves and those very unfashionable, hair style ruining caps you apply to your unsuspecting head to cushion the blow for any surviving curls when you suck in your skull and slip it into the helmet. Next I spent several minutes fiddling around with the helmet buckle and then out the door we went.

My chivalrous man started my snowmobile and then started his. We planted our amply covered rumps on our corresponding seats and slowly squeezed the throttles. He was most likely two tenths of a mile away before he realized I wasn't behind him. The helmet was a new experience for me and the combination of my anticipation and the "dog like" panting I was simulating caused some major fog inside the shield covering my face. I stopped and tried to wipe it off. I drove 20 feet and then stopped and wiped the visor clear again. It's best I do not give a detailed account of what I was thinking about then as it wasn't nice or lady like in any way.

Eventually I decided seeing where I was going wasn't nearly as important as I had originally thought so I just took off. It wasn't long before I realized snowmobiling is much less daunting if you can't see what's coming! Before long we had arrived at our destination. It's a safe two mile drive from town that contains no "tippy" spots where I'm forced to lean sideways along the side of the ditch. Mr. Knievel whizzed past me, by me, alongside me and over the top of me and observed my "butt leaving seat" moments when I hit some drifts that closely resembled the consistency of concrete. It was a rather brisk and somewhat windy day with temps -10 below zero and after several passes on my now favorite track I could hear small voices that appeared to be coming from the insides of my gloves. Those voices were saying, "Hellooooo! What are you trying to do to us?" Those voices were my fingertips. They were the only part of my flesh that decided to rebel and they stated their case very loudly and very clearly. Don stopped and after learning that my fingers weren't staying warm enough on my heated handlebars, he stepped off his sled and said, "Here, ride this sled for a while and see if these handlebars warm up your fingers."

The handlebars on his sled were indeed warmer but they presented a new situation I learned I would have to deal with immediately. The horse power in his sled and mine are somewhat different. When you squeeze the throttle on mine, eventually you start to move. When you squeeze the throttle on his the "eventually" is not part of the equation. The issue with the warmer handlebars isn't with the handlebars themselves but with the ability to hang onto them once you allow the throttle to tell the motor it's time to move!

Needless to say, I survived. This was only my second snowmobile riding adventure and so far I haven't lost control of my sled, I haven't tipped over and I haven't ran into anything or anyone. I did get a little too "up close and personal" with a tree branch but thankfully the rest of the tree was behind the fence I nearly got hung up in so that helped. I learned that panting is not the recommended breathing technique one should use when encased in a helmet equipped with a visor no matter how nervous you are, I learned that when Don stops his sled and climbs off of it to look back to see where I am and he's in snow up to his gonads I should listen to my gut when my guts says, "DON'T FOLLOW HIM!"

Heart "Strings"

When my first marriage ended I took a leap of faith. Translated that means I asked if my mother would rent me my old bedroom until I decided what my plan of real action would be. It wasn't ideal as she treated me as if I was 16 so it took a while before I embraced her thrill for the chance to "mother" me once again. Looking back, I wouldn't trade it for anything in the world.

She had redecorated the bedroom I had when I was growing up and it wasn't long before I asked for her permission to tone things down a bit. Every corner of the room vividly displayed

195

splashes of incredibly bright pink. There were pink curtains, a pink comforter, a pink chair, pink throw rugs and pink pillows. When the sun shine rolled through the windows at sundown it even looked as if the walls were pink. She chose this cheerful color when she decided to sleep in this room again for a while after dad passed away. It took her a while before she could go back to their bedroom as it felt so empty without him there. Thankfully by the time I wanted to rent it she was back in the room she shared with dad and didn't mind my request for a change.

I decided on a nice shade of taupe for the walls and accented with shades of brown and slate blue and once everything was finished it became the tranquil place I needed at the end of the 12 hour days I was working. I remember the day when I decided to wash the sheets. As I was stripping the bed I found several blankets and a comforter under the sheet used to add a bit of padding to the worn mattress they were covering. This wasn't anything I hadn't seen before as we always had to make things last as long as possible. Money was never in abundance when I was growing up so a mattress that could be "padded" surely didn't need to be replaced. Like I said, this wasn't anything I hadn't seen before, however, as I rolled the blankets away I saw long threads attached to the comforter. My curiosity convinced me to investigate and this is the story that followed. It will always make me smile.

"Well Bev, years ago when your sister went to work at the post office I babysat with April." April is my sister's youngest daughter and my Goddaughter. "She was so fun to have around and never the slightest bit of trouble. We would play and make bread dough and cookies and one day I taught her how to sew with a needle and thread. She was young but so smart and it wasn't long before she knew just exactly how to thread that needle and weave it in and out of fabric. I remember the day the reason for your question took place very well. I got busy in the kitchen and all of a sudden I realized April had been awfully quiet. I called out for her and it didn't take long for me to realize she was in my bedroom with the door shut. I asked her what she was doing and when she said she was just playing I knew she was fine. She didn't make any messes and she was such a good girl so I knew I didn't need to be worried. Eventually she came out of my bedroom and when I got the chance, I took a peek in there and everything seemed fine. We went about the rest of our day before her mom picked her up and it wasn't until bedtime that I realized what she was doing in my bedroom earlier that day. At first I was confused because as I went to pull the covers back on my bed I was met with a bit of resistance. I was confused, that is, until I did a quick investigation and learned that April had sewn my bed shut!

I just didn't have the heart to remove those strings as they always took me back to when April was a little girl and honestly, they were some of the best years of my life."

Love Never Fails

I've only been subjected to three emergency room visits in my lifetime and the first one happened before I was 2 years old and I don't remember it. The second one happened a very long time ago and the details are a bit hazy but the reasons for going there were more about pain that couldn't wait until the clinic opened the following day and less about me losing the beat in my heart. The third trip, however, is quite fresh in my mind, as it happened just the other night and as I sat waiting patiently for my name to be called I managed to gather some rather interesting material for my book.

When I entered the premises I scared the living day lights out of the receptionist that was busy dozing off while trying to make it look like she was reading a book. She nervously slid a form under the open area between the glass and the counter separating her from me and then asked me to take a seat once the pertinent information had been disclosed. Apparently things had been a little slow up until I arrived and I was only there because of a reaction I was experiencing from my doctor's third attempt to medicate my slightly elevated blood pressure. This particular pill has several typical side effects but the one I landed was at the very bottom of the side effects list in the "rare but severe" section. My lips turned into something that resembled two of those long balloons clowns use to concoct animals for children at birthday parties. Eventually my cheeks joined in and over the course of the day my face began to resemble one of those puzzles where the wrong top and wrong bottom were put together. From the nose up I looked pretty normal but from below the nose down it looked like I was attempting to hide the Goodyear Blimp inside my mouth!

Prior to my arrival there was a considerable amount of deliberation that included nudges from Don via phone as he was hundreds of miles away for work, the doctor's office nurse that decided not to wait until the following day to return my call, my brother and my sister so I finally caved and took myself in. It was feared that the swelling that had been wreaking havoc with my face all day might eventually decide to inhabit a space inside my tongue and possibly my throat. I did a short imaginary video of how things might play out if this happened while I was sleeping and I decided I wasn't incredibly happy with the end result. I can't say I'll be happy when the bill arrives but the experience was not boring.

Shortly after I arrived a woman came running in the door and pleaded with the slightly frazzled receptionist I had freaked out earlier by saying, "I have to get in there to be with my sister! She's alone and she's not having a seizure! She took an overdose of Valium! Oh, please let me go back there with her so I can tell the doctor what's wrong!" The receptionist was completely awake at this point and sitting rather straight in her chair and you could almost tell she was wondering if the woman on the other side of the counter was going to try and cram herself through the small slot I had slipped the paper with my pertinent information through earlier. It would have been one of those thrilling popcorn crunching moments you sometimes find yourself completely engulfed in at the movies but this wasn't a movie, it was reality and once the woman calmed down they took her back to be with her sister.

The sequel arrived moments later. She was a very tall, raw boned woman with short white hair. She was cussing when she walked in the door. She was cussing when she sat down two rows of chairs away from me and she cussed out that damn husband of hers the whole time she told me how clumsy he can be. I learned that the klutz was a man she had been married to for 65 years. I learned that he was on blood thinners and that his sense of balance leaves a lot to be desired and that the old fool should know better than to kick a door stop out of the way. She said, "He knows he falls every time he attempts to stand on one foot. The old fool. Now he has a big horn sticking out of his forehead and he's bleeding all over the damn place. I could just kill him right now."

After the frantic sister was taken back to be with her sister and the elderly woman was taken back to be with her "old fool" I couldn't help but think about all the ways love is portrayed. Sometimes it's hugs and kisses and tons of romance. Sometimes it's flowers when they're least expected, but sometimes it's making an attempt to be with someone you dearly love even if it means yelling and screaming at a powerless receptionist and sometimes it disguises itself by appearing to be angry and frustrated with the one person that means the world to you.

Love isn't always patient and kind. Sometimes it's packed with fear of losing someone near and dear to your heart. Sometimes it says things it doesn't mean but the one thing about love I do know for sure is....Love Never Fails.

Fabric Store Shopping Tips

The Top 10 Guidelines Shoppers Should Follow To Make Their Fabric Store Experience Rewarding For Themselves And Everyone Else In The Store Including The Employees:

1. If you've let your kids overdose on sugar, leave them home. Our walls are already taken by the overworked employees bouncing off of them and we have no other wall space available for your kids.

2. If your baby is ready for a nap wait until he/she has had that nap before heading to the store if you plan to bring them along. We understand random non-nap related outbursts but if you know Junior is beyond tired and ready to blow a gasket, save us all the torture of listening to him

scream non-stop for 20 minutes and let him have his nap first.

3. If you remove a bolt of fabric from somewhere and decide you don't want it, surprise every one of us and put it back where you found it and if you really want to go above and beyond, don't put it back on the rack upside down. I guarantee, this will shock employees...it may even kill a few of us.

4. If you decide you don't want something you've had riding around in your cart and you don't want to put it back where you found it, bring it to the registers or the cutting counter. Please don't just toss it onto any random flat surface it won't fall off of before you can make your get-away.

5. Please plan your shopping trip so that you're finished by the time the store closes. We employees never forget those of you that make us stay late and we have ways of making you pay and you won't even know it's happening.

6. If you regularly poop beside your toilet at your house, please return to your old habits once you're back home. We really don't like to clean up your poop, ever. (Yes, this really happens.)

7. If you must bring a beverage with you to the store, please toss it into one of the 9 garbage cans in the store once you're finished with it rather than stash it behind or under something. Would you want us to come to your house and leave our garbage in your linen closet or set it under your bed?

8. If you bring your school age children that have not overdosed on sugar with you please know where they are at all times and please don't let them convince you that they are not messing up the thread. They are. It's one of their favorite things to do.

9. If you are trying to match up 37 fabrics for a quilt please don't leave the 23 you decided against on the floor. Someone has to pick them up eventually and they don't like doing it as much you might think.

10. You're an adult and if you forget your coupons or your phone at home, don't whine to us, don't give us your best puppy dog eyes and don't make us feel bad because you messed up.

Most of the following things happen within a days' time, every day. I've had people sound as if they almost envy my "easy, relaxed, stress free" job. I'm just glad I have a fairly decent sense of humor because we all know violence just isn't the answer......no......it isn't.

A Restored Outlook

Life is such an interesting process, isn't it? We're born and from that moment on our bodies and minds begin to grow and change as each day comes and goes. Before long we find ourselves glancing back over those years reflecting on the experiences and relationships that have shaped the person we've become and if you're like me, you have memories of people that have changed you forever.

One of those people for me was a woman that became the janitor at the post office where I worked. She wasn't just any woman. She was a devout Catholic. She was never married and she formed relationships with almost no one. She was probably in her late sixties when she started her job at the post office and it was then I was given the opportunity to know more about this very private, lonely woman than anyone most likely ever had. Her story isn't long and complicated but it's sad. She told me about some of the reasons she had for acting the way she did and they broke my heart.

She was born into a family with several male siblings and was told at a very young age she had no value because she wasn't a boy. The most unfortunate part of what she was told is the fact that she believed it. What it did to her wasn't pretty or "socially acceptable" on the outside as she learned to avoid as much direct contact with people as she could. If you saw her walking down the street, she would always look away or straight down at the ground and she would never wave. She rented an apartment but due to circumstances she couldn't fully grasp, she was asked to leave. The landlord had very valid reasons for this request but it left her homeless. She was okay with that and I tried to help her figure out a place to live but was told rather sternly on more than one occasion, not to get involved. It wasn't easy but the community had some very kind and concerned souls that helped her with this life changing event and after several months of living away from her home town she returned to a crisp, clean, private room at the nursing home. It became very evident that she wasn't taking good care of herself while living in her apartment and the intervention became incredibly necessary. She didn't see it that way and I'll never forget the day she came back to her janitor job. I told her how happy I was to see her and with the most hollow and empty look on a face that I had ever seen she said, "I would rather be dead."

She hated that her apartment was taken away from her. She didn't understand why she had to stay at the nursing home because she was convinced she could take care of herself. I knew she wasn't capable of handling those responsibilities but I humored her and gave her a shoulder to cry on and then I did something that changed something in both of us forever.

I can't remember the timeline but I would venture to say it was most likely several weeks later when I saw a face that no longer displayed a hollow, empty look but rather a face filled with joy. I no longer saw someone pushing a broom across the floor as if they were attempting to move a mountain but rather a person that looked as if she was enjoying life and I said, "You're sure in a good mood today!" And she said, "The sun is shining, I'm alive and life is good!"

Prayers are answered. I'm not saying I'm the only one that prayed for this lost and lonely soul but I added mine to many others and what I witnessed was something I'll never forget. It didn't change who she was or what she believed but it did remove the ache in her heart and gave her a reason to smile.

It's never the big things…..the most precious gifts in life are and will always be…..the little things.

Brisk Empowering Steps

Life is such a fascinating process. If I had a dime for every time I've uttered those words I probably wouldn't be a very rich woman but I'd have a rather enormous pile of dimes.

At times I ponder all the amazing moments that have arrived in my life and all the experience I've gained and I sometimes wonder why I still say I'm not sure what I want to be when I grow up. At times I think about all the people that have entered into my life. Some were there for reasons and they've moved on. Some have been there my entire life and then others arrive with a spirited nature that, at times, force me to fluff and refold the ideas I've kept safely tucked in my somewhat stubborn half Norwegian half Scottish brain.

Several days ago Don and I were staying with my mother and I actually got up before both of them. I ate my breakfast while sitting in the very same spot my dad used to eat his breakfast for well over thirty years. I peered out the same window and as I sat there I couldn't help but think about all those mornings dad sat there. He would peer out that window and if anyone said anything to him it took a while before his thoughts were jolted away from where they were. What did he think about? He would usually sit there for quite a while but then, eventually he would get up and begin his day and he always accomplished something. For a moment I thought about being lazy and accomplishing absolutely nothing. I finally had a day off and our dirty laundry and carpets in need of vacuuming were over 200 miles away but then, something happened. A total shift in my thoughts. Before long I had a plan. I washed mom's dishes, rounded up her garbage and cleaned the bathroom. Once finished I found myself scrounging around for some nice warm clothes that were about to be talked into going for a rather brisk Saturday morning walk with me. It had been a while since my four mile a day walks so I decided to give a two mile walk a try.

As I headed down the quiet little road that brings people into this lovely little community I was overwhelmed with the peace I felt. It was the kind of peace that I experience only when I choose to set aside some time for myself and when this happens I'm reminded that I'm never completely alone. I could feel the Lord's presence so strongly that every once in a while I stopped to look back and at one point I watched as my shadow inched it's way along expecting to see another right there beside me. It was then I realized it was time to let go of some things. It was time to stop feeling guilty for making some very necessary changes in my life. I think I finally believe guilt is pointless. It was then I realized we can only be happy when we truly believe we are unique and that we have value and no one can create that belief within us for us. We are all on our very own journey. We learn throughout our lifetime that the only way we can be a blessing to others is to believe that we too, are a blessing. We torture ourselves with feelings of unworthiness and inadequacy and serve ourselves heaping helpings of stress without ever realizing we will never be able to digest it all. Slowly our bodies respond to that gluttony and eventually it takes its toll.

Some might find it hard to believe what power a brisk Saturday morning walk may potentially have but for a woman that feels as if she has finally found her way after being lost for so many years, I must say, it was empowering!

Analytical Stones

Our journeys are all different. We meet so many people and I believe they all, in some way, have had an impact on where we've been, where we are or where we'll find ourselves as our story continues.

I was visiting with a dear friend yesterday and her journey has taken her to a place where she is forcing herself to be courageous. She's endured numerous surgeries to remove the unhealthy cells that took root and grew in her unsuspecting flesh. This woman is among a small percentage of people in my journey that have shown me the kind of friendship you don't establish with everyone you choose to call your friend. Her heart is filled with compassion. Her eyes sparkle and shine and every time I've visited with her, I feel a genuine sense of her immeasurable love for others.

The conversation we had yesterday involved her experience with someone that had a very negative impact on me several years ago. I learned that this person is now weaving her distorted reality into the minds of unsuspecting souls at the expense of my dear friend. She's very good at what she does and during my experience with her, my path was very lonely. I tried to expose her dishonesty and lack of integrity but I never felt as if anyone would ever believe me but were convinced rather, that I was the one that needed to make some positive changes in my life.

My analytical mind tends to work overtime and I search endlessly for reasons hurtful behaviors or circumstances present themselves at the worst possible times. Here is what I have so far.

I honestly believe they're meant to be distractions. They cause our minds to shift our focus at times, and most often, when our minds are fixated on something painful or frightening we are forced to endure. During my "not so pleasant" experience with the woman mentioned earlier, I realized my marriage was no longer a marriage. Did the lies she told about me help? Probably not but they definitely put a bit more fist in my fight and grit in my sight. Not long after my dad passed away the house my mom is living in began to fall apart. The sink stopped up, the toilet quit working, the water heater went out, the septic tank needed to be dug up, the basement flooded, the electrical box had to be relocated, the water line started leaking and the transmission went out on her car! She missed dad terribly but she didn't have quite as much time to think about him as she thought she needed as she was too busy trying to keep up with all the disasters going on around her.

My dear friend shared her story with me because she knew I had been there, in that same place, several years ago. I've since moved on and chosen a new direction. I'm traveling a path that has led me to some amazing places and I'm a better person because of it. I prayed for my dear friend last night and I'll continue to pray for her. I also prayed for the woman that continues to find ways to put as many bumps in other's roads as she possibly can. Those capable of hurting others are just covering pain they harbor within themselves. They've lost their way and no matter how much effort they put into "throwing stones" at others, I pray they'll one day realize those "stones" will never pave a path in the right direction.

Diminished Abilities

I've known my mother for fifty years but today, she said four words I have never heard her say in all those fifty years and it tore a hole in my heart. When she called she said, "Hi Bev! I'm so happy to hear your voice! So you got the day off." I said, "Yes, I sure did and it's nice to hear your voice too! How are you doing today?" And then those four words arrived and I could feel the tears forming in my eyes and in my heart. She said, "I'm kind of lonely."

For nine months prior to my arrival I listened to her beating heart each and every second of each and every day. Our bond is one of the most precious gifts I have ever received and it's a gift I will cherish until the beating of my very own heart comes to an end.

In her earlier years, she was one of the most ambitious people I knew. She was always doing something and it was usually something that involved the use of her young, strong arms and her two strong legs. Her life wasn't easy but I don't ever remember her complaining when she lugged dirty laundry down two flights of stairs twice a week to an old ringer type washing machine. Every Monday and every Thursday she would fill that old washing machine and the old galvanized tub with water that would later create numerous buckets of dirty water she would have to carry back upstairs to dump. I don't ever remember her complaining as she ironed mountains of clean clothes that always included those navy blue and red hankies dad carried in his pockets. As I got a little older she would let me iron those. For some reason she made ironing look kind of fun so it was always a treat to get to do the hankies. My mom never assigned chores. She never forced an established bed time on us. She never told us we were lazy and she never got upset when something ended up broken. She just created an atmosphere of happiness and led three kids into adulthood with all the necessary tools they would need to build that very same warm and comfortable existence and not once do I ever remember her slowing down long enough to let loneliness get it's grips on her.

She's eighty years old now and each day a small part of her independence is being taken away. She has moments when those losses take their toll and she says things she really doesn't mean. She struggles with a lot of tasks she used to do with ease and her patience is tested time and time again. She tells me that it isn't easy to get old. She tells me that she feels like she's fifty on the inside but her body sees things considerably different and then she tells me how nice it would be if she could see me every day. Occasionally she tells me about all the things she is still able to do but the list is getting shorter with each passing day and the unwelcome stranger she has managed to avoid nearly every day of her life is finding its way into her world with each bit of ability fate is taking away.

I'm not sure if she realizes it, but I'm still learning things from her. I'm learning that the will to survive may someday be the strongest part of who I am. I'm learning that there is something to be thankful for each and every day. I'm learning that we should take absolutely nothing for granted and that we should be thankful for even the tiniest of blessings.

A while back, during a discussion that involved my strategy for managing certain circumstances I was told that perhaps I was "just too nice." If that's possible, it's who I strive to be. If it's true, it's most likely a big part of the reason I'm not farther ahead in life but if those three little words are really what defines me, my mother did indeed, accomplish what she set out to do.

Celebrating The Little Things

There is a gnat keeping me company at the moment. It's probably one of the smallest I have ever seen in my entire life which is making it incredibly hard to catch between my two outstretched palms. A few seconds ago it landed on the computer screen giving me an opportunity to remove it from my presence but I didn't. I sat there and stared at it. It started hovering around my screen again and it will most likely drive me bananas but a part of me sat here completely amazed at how something so tiny could be alive and have wings and the ability to dodge two palms more than a dozen time that were several hundred times larger.

Some may find it odd but there are a lot of little things in this world that amaze me. I'm not always tickled pink about them, especially if they're a microscopic gnat that continues to dance around in my face but there are just a whole lot of fascinating details provided to us daily that are incredibly easy to miss if we're not willing to give up a small amount of our time. Have you ever set aside a few minutes to sit down with your niece to watch how her pet butterfly sucks sugar water out of a napkin? It's so cool. And have you ever tasted the nectar at the bottom of a honeysuckle blossom? It's sweeter than you would ever believe. Have you ever had your mother tell you that she really wonders if you'll ever look old when you were two weeks away from celebrating your 50th birthday? It's something I'll never forget. And have you ever sent someone a text that read, "Have I told you lately...." and before you had a chance to send the second text with the rest of that thought, you receive a text that says, "I love you more!"

It's easy to get caught up in the day to day struggles and juggles life has a tendency to deliver but it doesn't mean there isn't time to slow the pace, break the rules, really listen to what someone has to say every once in a while and maybe, just maybe, let someone finish your sentences. It might end up revealing one of the sweetest, box-less, unwrapped, untied, bow-less gifts you'll ever receive!

Two Wrongs - One Right

I'm not sure why but for as long as I can remember I find myself making attempts to discover what lies beyond the surface of the people I know, the people I meet and the people I love. I always wonder what actually makes them tick. The ones that warrant the bulk of my attention are the angry ones and the dreamers.

My dad was one of the angry ones. I'm thankful that God gave me just over 40 years to ponder the reasons why he seemed so angry and over the course of those 40 years I learned that he really wasn't angry at all. He was wounded. He had to say goodbye to his mom when he was 5 years old as cancer treatments weren't nearly as advanced back then as they are now. He found out very quickly that nothing in his life would ever be the same. I'll never forget the day he opened up to me in his room at the nursing home. He told me he built a shield of armor around himself when he was very young and there was no way anyone, and he emphasized ANYONE, would be able to hurt him. He learned that he would probably always have to rely on himself and that is how he perceived his future. I miss my dad. He was stern and sometimes scary in the eyes of a little kid, especially when some of his "pain" slipped out. We heard it loudly and clearly but we respected him. He always made us feel safe and always provided for us no matter how hard it was as we were growing up. I loved my dad and as I savor the memories of his presence in my life I've realized just how much he loved me too.

I work with a young gal and she would fall into the category of the dreamers. As I mentioned earlier, dreamers are also souls that warrant the bulk of my attention. I met her nearly three years ago and I'll never forget that day. She was assigned to help me cover all of my working surfaces in my frame shop with cardboard so that over time, as the cardboard got worn and torn, it could be easily replaced. I knew the very second I met her that she had a story that I wanted to hear.

We opened our brand new store at the very end of October back in 2015. Veronica was chosen to work as a framer in my shop but over time her potential for success was better recognized when she was helping customers out on the floor. She has an overwhelming desire to help others and she'll stop at almost nothing to help a customer find exactly what they are looking for. The relationship I have with her has evolved greatly over the past three years but it wasn't until recently that I was able to understand what makes her "tick."

She was notorious for blurting out things almost as if she had a conversation going on in her head a bit before she started talking. I hate to say it but there were times this caused me a bit of frustration. As it began happening more and more I finally decided I needed to stop her and ask if she would go back a few "thought" steps. She never took offense but rather giggled and helped me to understand what she had originally been trying to communicate. The process of stopping her and backing her up went on for quite some time and I couldn't help but think there was more to her story and that perhaps, if I was patient, she may just offer me more backward "thought" steps.

As time went on Veronica appeared to be spending more time in the frame shop visiting with me when she had a few extra minutes and there is one day, in particular, that I will never forget as long as I live. This was the day the beautiful dreamer revealed a very important link that made every bit of her "dreaminess" amazingly clear.

I'm not sure how we got on the subject of her parents but I knew from past conversations that she and they were never close. She remembers her dad making fun of her and pointing out her flaws. She hasn't seen him for a very long time and hasn't found a good reason to drive to the prison he's been residing in for years. Her mother had no desire to bond with her so the relationship a child longs for with at least one parent was never a part of her reality. She never had enough to eat and always had to look after her little brothers so her mom could enjoy her freedom.

As I made an attempt to digest the horrific childhood this incredibly kind hearted young woman had experienced, I found myself wondering just how a child is able to triumph over such heart wrenching circumstances. My mom was my most favorite person on the face of this earth. Her love was some of the most beautiful love I would ever know and the thought of never having experienced this was nearly unfathomable for me. I knew I had to ask Veronica how she was able to survive in a home without love and when I did this was her response. "I created an imaginary friend. I named her Yoko. I talked to her. I loved her and she loved me." At that moment I think my heart stopped beating. Everything about this young woman finally made sense. The conversations she appeared to have always started before she opened her mouth stemmed from all those years when she had conversations with Yoko.

Veronica is a delightful person. You would never see any of the pain that must exist in her somewhere if you ever had the pleasure of meeting her. She works harder than anyone I know and is one of the most resilient souls I have ever met. She could be bitter but she isn't. She could be angry but she isn't. She could have been someone just like the two people that created her but she proved to me that two wrongs definitely made one right.

Answers

Do you pray? And if you do, do you believe it will be answered?

I pray. I don't always see dramatic results but every once in a while I do. I think God can tell when we're ready to see some big changes. They don't always come without cost but they give us reason to believe that anything is possible and they restore wavering faith and hope when life gives us the feeling things will never change for the better.

I'm 54 years old and I still joke about "what I'll be when I grow up." Have you ever done that? Even though it's typically followed by laughter and a big smile, it causes me to wonder why. At times I allow myself to ponder on all the things that could have been but each and every time I reach the very same conclusion. I've lived. I've loved and I've done my best. God puts those conclusions in there for me. He knows I'm living out my life in the way He intended. He just sometimes has a hard time helping me to believe every second of every day has had value. I've touched a few hearts. I've listened to my own and I know great things are coming. Great things like believing in myself and knowing that no matter what life gives me or what life takes away, I matter. I've swept floors and ironed piles of laundry. I've scrubbed stains out of towels at a hotel that should have been thrown away. I've stood all day for days on feet that are screaming for relief. I've worked three jobs so that I could pave the path for something better when making everyone else happy just wasn't enough anymore.

This isn't about my life. It's about everyone's life. We all have times when we need to believe we're here for a reason. We all have times when life drags us down and forces us back to our very foundation so that we remember what really matters. It isn't about money. It isn't about things. It isn't about having the best of everything. It's about having a love and peace filled heart that doesn't need to be reminded to pray only when something bad happens.

Thanks for being a part of my journey. I'm glad our paths crossed. Have a love and faith filled day and know you are never alone.

If you managed to navigate your way through the 216 pages before you read this page it is safe to say,

"You've Been Bevitized!"

My husband came up with the name for this book without realizing it. He had lived alone for a number of years before we met and had settled quite nicely into his "bachelor pad." There were 208 miles between his driveway and mine which meant we kept automobile service departments and gas stations in business for quite a while. Every other weekend when it was my turn to head his direction I would rearrange a few things in his house giving him a preview of what he could expect when I actually moved in. He referred to this as "Bevitizing" his world. When I started writing it wasn't at all difficult to decide what a collection of stories gathered by my whimsical and sometimes doltish brain should wear as its title.

I just believe we are all so incredibly You-nique and the special gifts we're blessed with were meant to be shared with the world. Thanks so much for allowing me to share my love and perception of the world with you.

May you always be blessed in ways beyond your vantage point.

May you gain immeasurable wisdom throughout your life that you'll willingly share with others and may your life be filled with the peace and love of our most Amazing Lord and Savior, Jesus Christ.